TAUGHT
BY THE
SPIRIT

TAUGHT BY THE SPIRIT

by
RON AUCH

New Leaf Press

Typesetting by: Total Type & Graphics
                   Berryville, AR 72616

Library of Congress Catalog Number: 90-64184
ISBN: 0-89221-191-1

DEDICATION

To my son Ronnie. He has taught me the importance of relationships. His influence on me has deeply impacted my life as well as my relationship with God.

ACKNOWLEDGMENT

Thanks must go to John Cronce once again for his assistance with the manuscript. His "touch" is evident throughout.

Thanks also to Geri Auch, who types tirelessly to help us meet our deadline.

CONTENTS

1. Taught by the Spirit 11

2. Be Still and Know 25

3. The Offense of the Cross 41

4. The Spirit of Harlotry 49

5. Children of Harlotry 57

6. Isaac vs. Ishmael 71

7. The Adulterous Generation 89

8. Controlling Spirits 105

9. Worshipolatry 129

10. Violent Men 153

11. Plain Men of God 165

12. Men of the Presence 181

13. Clear Conscience 193

14. Closet Prayer 211

15. The Spirit of Prayer 219

ONE

TAUGHT BY THE SPIRIT

There are some things man cannot do,
and these he should not try to accomplish.
He must learn that some tasks are the
exclusive domain of his Creator.
—President Andrew Johnson

I shifted uneasily in my favorite easy chair as the televangelist I was watching continued his message. And it wasn't getting any better. If anything, it was growing worse. He had been explaining (at great length) how most pastors don't teach the truth. Now he was encouraging his viewers to disregard the teachings of most pastors (and the pastors themselves) because they were untrue. It seemed to me as if he was trying to convince people to reject their pastors and listen only to him (which would ultimately have the effect of him receiving their tithes). I don't know if his motivations were purely monetary or not, but I am absolutely positive that his message was in error. Like most erroneous doctrines, his was based on Scripture; or more precisely, on a misinterpretation of Scripture.

> And as for you, the anointing which you have received from Him abides in you, and you have no need for anyone to teach you; but as His anointing teaches you about all things, and is true and is not a lie, and just as it has taught you, you abide in Him (1 John 2:27).

The evangelist I saw used this verse to substantiate his message. He claimed that this verse proves that the Holy Spirit is the only teacher we need, and he further alleged that this implies that we don't need a pastor. It was his contention that believers need only to read their Bibles and allow the Holy Spirit to teach them. But if that is true, then we must erase the following words from the pages of Scripture:

> And He gave some as apostles, and some as prophets, and some evangelists, and some as pastors, and teachers (Eph. 4:11).

God Himself ordained the offices of the pastor and the teacher every bit as much as he ordained the other positions mentioned in that verse (including that of the evangelist). How then can mere man say that pastors and teachers aren't needed? Clearly we do need them. The Holy Spirit isn't supposed to replace them. He actually functions in tandem with them. He will speak to our hearts, telling us whether or not the teacher we are listening to is speaking truth. According to Romans 8:16, the Spirit of God will bear witness with our spirit whether something is truth or a lie. He confirms whether what is being said or done is really of God. But He won't use a Holy Spirit hypodermic to inject us with information about God. Teachers and pastors provide us with information about God, as does our own personal time in God's Word. The Holy Spirit confirms or denies the legitimacy of the information we receive.

His role in interpreting Scripture and teaching about the nature of God is crucial. Without Him, we can end up making Scripture mean anything we want. And there is only one way to get in tune with Him and with the spiritual realm: through prayer. Because of the very nature of God's Spirit, we cannot learn His ways or become sensitive to Him through any other means. Only in the presence of God does one begin to sense His nature. Our senses are trained by use, and prayer is the using or training of our senses.

> For though by this time, you ought to be teachers, you have need again for someone to teach you the elementary principles of the oracles of God, and you have come to need milk and not solid food. For everyone who partakes only of milk is not accustomed to the word of righteousness, for he is a babe. But solid food is for the mature, who because of practice have their senses trained to discern good and evil (Heb. 5:12-14).

When God Speaks

All through the Bible, we read of God speaking to His people when they were in prayer. Daniel had been in prayer for three weeks when the angel came with the revelation of his vision (Daniel 10:2-5). When God called Moses to the mountain to give him the Ten Commandments, He told him to go and "be there." Moses was there for seven days before God spoke to Him and revealed the Ten Commandments. When Moses got to the top, the cloud covered the mountain

13

and the glory of the Lord rested on Mount Sinai (Exodus 12:12-16). I think we can safely assume Moses spent those seven days in prayer before God revealed the Law to Moses. After all, what else would the average patriarch have done in such a setting?

God has always revealed Himself after man sought Him. Today we have the complete Word of God, so we needn't seek Him to get something to add to the Bible. However, we still need the inner witness of the Spirit to help us identify truth. That inner witness is developed through spending time with Jesus and by no other way. A strict study of God's Word won't produce it. You will experience it only as a result of a combination of prayer and a study of the Bible, the emphasis being on prayer first.

Why prayer first? Because prayer tips the balance in the battle between our spirit and flesh. The Scripture indicates that we are in a constant struggle between two natures.

> For the flesh sets its desire against the Spirit, and the Spirit against the flesh; for these are in opposition to one another... (Gal. 5:17).

We need to bring the flesh into submission to the Spirit, otherwise the flesh will dominate our interpretation of the Scripture. Prayer does this. In prayer, the influence of our flesh is squelched. This is caused by something called repentance, which is the death of the flesh. You can't avoid it when you're in God's presence. In fact, the whole process of prayer is the development of repentance. When a person sincerely spends time in God's presence, he can't help but begin to clean house. He starts to see things from God's perspective, not just from man's. The more time he spends in His presence, the more he begins to think like God. He deals with more and more issues in his life that require repentance. Without consistency in prayer, there are some issues we will never deal with.

We shall know by this that we are of the truth, and shall assure our heart before Him in whatever our heart condemns us for God is greater than our heart, and knows all things (1 John 3:19,20).

Once a man brings his flesh into submission, God then can begin to reveal things about His nature and Word that He could not have revealed before. That's why prayer is pre-eminent. A man must know God before He will receive great revelation.

Where Do Revivals Come From?

The thought of God revealing Himself to a man is as fantastic as it is life-changing. Consider Paul, the apostle, on the road to Damascus. If that is what happens to one individual, think of what happens when the whole Church begins to pray and seek God, ultimately receiving a revelation of Him. That's the earliest stirrings of revival. When the Church spends much time praying, it begins to see what God does and does not approve of, and through that people are led to repentance. They turn from their former ways and begin doing the things God approves of, and they abstain from things God disapproves of. But that's still just the beginning. It's the repentance of the Church as a whole that leads to revival. As the revival sweeps the land, even non-Christians begin to repent. Soon you have a mighty move of God in the country. It all starts with prayer, and it all continues in prayer. Prayer starts the revival and prayer sustains it.

The repentant heart characterizes any revival. It highlighted the First Great Awakening, the Second Great Awakening, and every other move of God we know of. The repentant heart was a catalyst for much of what happened. This is because a repentant heart yields the purest doctrines available, but because sincerely repentant hearts are seen almost exclusively during revival, that's also where the purest doctrines are found. Doctrine developed during revival is a doctrine formulated around the Spirit having precedence over the flesh. Doctrine developed in days that are far removed from revival (and subsequently repentance) tends to cater to the flesh. This is why we have such a fleshly church today. We have left the ancient boundaries. We have neglected the admonishment of Proverbs 22:28 which states, "Do not remove the ancient boundary which your fathers have set." The forefathers of each move of God established the boundaries and convictions for their movement from prayer. Today the ancient boundaries are little more than nostalgia as we set about to indulge our flesh. We have departed from the pure doctrine that was born of the Spirit during the revival and have adopted our own doctrine born out of a desire of the flesh.

Refiner's Fire

But who can endure the day of His coming? And who can stand when He appears? For He is like a refiner's fire and like fuller's soap. And He will sit as a smelter and purifier of silver and He will purify the sons of Levi and refine them like gold and silver, so that they may present to the Lord offerings in righteousness (Mal. 3:2,3).

Today, like never before, the Church needs the purifying that can only be brought by God's refining fire. Yet we are in the midst of the greatest material blessings the Church has ever known. We have grand buildings and impressive technology at our disposal. Yet we are filled with spiritual dross. Comfort and pleasure have seemingly become elevated above all other considerations. We have become a generation of entertainment and pleasure addicts and are losing out spiritually.

Our situation is really not that unique or remarkable, though. In times of abundance, people always seem to clutch to their material goods most. We seem unwilling to let go of the bobbles and trinkets God has permitted us to have. It's quite different when we face adversity. As soon as we have little or no material blessings, we run instinctively to God, praying fervently and yielding to Him what little we do have. However, these hard times aren't much of a test of our faith. Those times are just instances of us running to God only because we have no choice; we have no where else to run. The truest test of our faith is in the day of plenty, when God has blessed us with abundance.

Your commitment to the Lord can be measured by your prayer life. It can tell you if you really want God or if you want only the things God can give you. If you really want God, you pray just as much in good times as you do in the bad. But if you are really only interested in what God can give you, you will stop praying as soon as God has given you the latest thing you want. This is why you can't really tell much about your commitment to God during hard times. There's an old saying which was made into a popular song during World War II: There are no atheists in fox holes. Everyone will pray when they are desperate. But only someone truly committed to the Lord will pray when all appears to be going well.

Revival is the refiner's fire. Revival most often comes because of hard times. Hard times bring us to prayer. Prayer ultimately leads to repentance. Even if someone does not feel particularly repentant, but, seeing his spiritual need for repentance, does pray consistently anyway—God will work in his heart. All He asks for is humble people who will see their limitations and shortcomings and seek Him. God will bring them to repentance. The refiner's fire will purify those people, removing the dross from their lives. Their repentance will spark revival which, in turn, will lead to even more repentance. Repentance is the fuller's soap.

It is in this setting, where the dross (flesh) has been removed, God can speak to us more clearly than ever before. Our understanding of His Word is uncluttered by doctrines that cater to the flesh. That's when we become taught by the Spirit. When we hear a man preach, his words bear witness with our spirits. Deep down inside, we know whether he is preaching truth because of the Holy Spirit's nudging in our spirit. He won't permit us to be led astray by false doctrines.

But when we get away from prayer, we sacrifice all this. We lose our ability to discern whether a man is speaking the truth or not. The flesh begins to assume control once again, and we begin looking for doctrines that cater to our carnal desires. The old doctrines founded in prayer during revival are scorned. We hear statements like, "It's legalism to tell us we can't do that. That doctrine was for the old days. Times have changed. That used to be sin, but it's not sin today." Many of today's popular teachers/preachers simply espouse psychology.

Itching Ear

For the time will come when they will not endure sound doctrine; but wanting to have their ears tickled, they will accumulate for themselves teachers in accordance to their own desires; and will turn away their ears from the truth, and will turn aside to myths (2 Tim. 4:3,4).

In this letter, believed to have been written by Paul shortly before his death, the apostle gave his younger associate, Timothy, his final words of instruction. He told him to preach the Word, to reprove, to rebuke, and to give instruction—and Paul wrote this with an ominous prophecy looming in the background. In 2 Timothy 3, he warned that an apostate church would arise. It would be a church populated by evil men and wicked women who would be lovers of pleasure rather than lovers of God. They would be a people without self-control, malicious gossips who would not endure sound doctrine. The apostate believer has been described as a man who knows God (in our vernacular we would say he has been born again), but who will not let the truth that he knows, prompt him into any service for God. The apostate church will be crammed full of people who know God, but who will do nothing for Him. It will be a time of back yard barbecues and high-speed boats, but no service to God.

Importantly, Paul said these people would not endure sound doctrine. To endure means to suffer. Suffering is the very core of the gospel. Jesus learned obedience through the things he suffered (Hebrews 5:8), and in this context, it's not talking about the cross. It's talking about the self-denial He learned long before the cross. In other words, those who won't endure (suffer) sound doctrine, get away from the basic nature of the gospel. Instead of denying self, they cater to self. They enlist teachers who will preach the popular gospel of self-centeredness. They turn their ears away from the truth.

Consider how far we have come from the message of self-denial today. If a minister were to take a vow of poverty for the sake of the gospel today, he'd be laughed right out of the church. He would be told, "Don't you know that God wants you to be wealthy?" I find it ironic that many, though certainly not all, TV ministers are saying that the only reason they seek success from God is so they can turn around and bless God with it. They tell their viewers that if they need money, they should send money to them because then they'll receive ten or a hundred times back what they gave to the ministry. If they believed what they preached, they would announce on TV that anybody with a need could call in and ask for money knowing that the more money the ministry gave away, the more God would return to them one-hundred fold. It would be a way for God to meet their financial obligations without raising any skepticism from others. Today the Church does not believe its own message of sowing and reaping and is denying the message of self-denial.

A friend of mine who pastors in Florida was invited to lunch by another pastor in the same city. This particular minister had left his denomination to join the ranks of an independent group which promoted the "get rich quick" theology, and he wanted to know what my friend thought about it. My friend couldn't endorse it. "Why not?" the other pastor asked in mock astonishment. My friend reached into his jacket and opened his pocket New Testament. "Let me read a portion of scripture to you."

> For many walk, of whom I often told you, and now tell you even weeping, that they are enemies of the cross of Christ, whose end is destruction, whose god is their appetite, and whose glory is their shame, who set their minds on earthly things (Phil. 3:18,19).

After my friend finished reading, he put his New Testament back in his pocket. Then, looking the man across the table squarely in the eyes, he said as kindly as possible, "Your new doctrine is an enemy of the cross, and you could become an enemy of the cross of Christ through your doctrine's lack of self-denial. Your new theology causes us to set our minds on earthly things." He wasn't sure how the other pastor would respond to such frankness—some things are taken with great offense no matter how kindly you say them. But he never expected the response he got. A thin smile played on the corners of the other man's mouth. He began shaking his head in a barely perceptible way, as if offering pity. "Look," he said in his most ingratiating tone (one usually only employed by used car dealers), "you're young, you're good looking, you're sharp—you could be doing a lot better than you are now." My friend eyed him cautiously. "Consider this," he continued, pausing for effect. "There are only about 12,000 churches in your movement. If you were to join me, become an evangelist, I could get you into a network of one hundred thousand churches." He lowered his voice and flashed a brilliant smile, "Do you have any idea how much money you could make?" My friend was astonished. What he had read hadn't sunk in at all. In fact, it was if he never read the verse at all. That man was concerned only with how much money he could make. His appetite had become his god.

There is a very popular movement today that tickles the ear of the hearer. Proponents of this movement are not enemies of Christ, but are enemies of His cross. They are enemies of self-denial. Self has become their god and to deny self would be a sort of blasphemy of its own. They preach a message that all is well in a day when all is not well. In a day when the clarion call of the Church should be repentance, they are telling their listeners that God's only interest is blessing them. I recall hearing one preacher say, "I'm a blessings preacher. All I focus on is the blessings of God." I'll admit the blessings message gets a good response when an appeal for money is given. It's easy—and most often profitable—to preach what people want to hear, but we need someone to teach us the elementary principles of the oracles of God.

It's Show Time!

I remember teaching at a minister's conference in the Appalachian Mountains of Georgia where one of the pastors in attendance cryptically remarked, "I think our denomination should be called the T.G.T.G. Church." I asked him what the letters stood for, and he replied, "The Gadget That's Going. It seems that there is no genuine move of God's Spirit these days, so we're trying to make up one of our own. And our people seem to be satisfied with going to whoever has the biggest show in town." I almost think he understated the matter. What people really seem to be looking for is, in the words of P.T. Barnum, "the greatest show on earth." It's interesting how so much in the Church is promoted on a planetary basis, as if bigger is necessarily better. Nearly every conference we see advertised in Christian magazines emphasizes the fact that it's a world-wide conference. It may be a conference held in Hoboken, New Jersey that attracts only the local pastors and a few from New Hampshire, but it's almost sure to get the same bloated description that makes it sound like an international summit meeting. Under our current "tickle the ears" philosophy, everything must get bigger in order to get better.

I can see a variation on this theme as I recall teaching a seminar at a church in Utah that had a reputation for being some kind of revival center. I discovered that each Sunday night they would bring in a special speaker. Things were going great. Attendance was around 500 people. The pastor began to feel God speak to him about truly shepherding his people. After much prayer, he made the announcement that they were no longer going to have a special speaker each week and that they were going to concentrate on being a family unit. The next Sunday night, around 40 people showed up. The attendance remained between 40 and 80 for several years. Once he put an end to the carnival atmosphere and stopped featuring "gadgets," and started stressing commitment, the majority of his congregation lost interest. They moved elsewhere, doubtless to wherever the biggest show in town was.

The very essence of the Pentecostal heritage is that of witnessing powerful manifestations of God in the services. But because it has become lethargic in its prayer life and in seeking God, those manifestations are only rarely experienced. Now, faced with this lack, it seems to be counterfeiting those experiences. There was a time when Pentecostal believers, filled with the Holy Spirit, would dance before the

Lord, even as King David did. These were acts of spontaneity, completely inspired by God. That spontaneity and inspiration is missing in today's churches, so choreographed dancing has replaced it. If the Spirit gives life to something, it is proper and in order. But if the flesh gives life to something it is improper and sensual. This is certainly the case in this instance. I have spoken to men who have watched choreographed dancing, and they have said that the most pleasure they got out of it was watching women move around sensually.

People today don't seem to realize that Pentecostalism was always meant to be a response to the moving of the Holy Spirit. Today the Pentecostal realm seems to have developed a reliance on a technique of the business world; it's called franchising. When one man finds a successful program or gimmick, word of it gets around and everyone else tries to do the same thing. There is no spirit in it, God hasn't given birth to it, yet men strive mightily to reproduce it. We seem to have achieved (to our disgrace) what the scientific community has long aspired to do: we have perfected cloning.

The Pentecostal movement has traditionally stood out in sharp contrast to the Evangelical denominations. Its emphasis on the moving of God created an unbridgeable gap between the two groups. The Evangelicals' emphasis has been and continues to be intellectualism. Academia tends to be their Holy Spirit. They are limited to what they understand and to what conforms to their Aristotelian logic, and they have imposed the same limitations on God. They fail to realize that academia tends to center on man and his ability to understand. Academia therefore, breeds pride, and pride will not allow us to respond to God the way we should.

If prayer does not play a large part in our relationship with God, then doctrines of the flesh develop. Today we have abandoned the prayer closet and have subsequently developed doctrines that stink of carnality. It doesn't matter if it's the Pentecostal churches trying to manufacture the Holy Spirit or if it's the Evangelical churches depending on academia; both have a stench of carnality. Both are of the flesh. When the Church will not die to the flesh, then what we offer up to God as worship stinks. In Leviticus 16:25, we find that the fat of an animal was burned upon the altar. The fat went up as a sweet smelling savor to God. Only the burning of the fat or flesh goes up as something sweet smelling to God. When we refuse to lay carnality down on the altar, we cannot offer up to God a sweet smelling savor. Prayer is the laying down of carnality. If a man will give himself to God through prayer, God will begin to develop in his heart the doctrines and lifestyle that bring pleasure to Him, as He burns away the flesh.

TWO

BE STILL AND KNOW

Man strives mightily, but if he labors apart from God, his efforts will bring only frustrated activity. —Anonymous

God is our refuge and strength, an ever-present help in trouble. Therefore, we will not fear, though the earth give way and mountains fall into the heart of the sea, though its waters roar and foam and the mountains quake with their surging. There is a river whose streams make glad the city of God, the holy place where the Most High dwells. God is within her, she will not fall: God will help her at break of day. Nations are in uproar, kimgdoms fall: he lifts his voice, the earth melts. The Lord Almighty is with us. The God of Jacob is our fortress...Be still and know that I am God; I will be exalted among the nations, I will be exalted in the earth (Psa. 46:1-7,10).

God reveals Himself throughout the Scriptures as His people's source of strength. He knows how frail His people are and how easily they can be overcome by the circumstances of life, so He makes Himself and His strength available for them. He wants to be our refuge, an ever-present help in times of trouble. Certainly we live in a day of trouble, a day when nations are in uproar and kingdoms are falling. This is true in both the physical world and in the spiritual realm. The Church is under severe spiritual attack by the enemy.

So what are we supposed to do about it? According to God's Word, we are supposed to be still and know that God is God. We are to find inner spiritual tranquillity in the knowledge that our God is the omnipotent, omniscient, omnipresent Creator of all that is. There is nothing that He cannot accomplish. There isn't even anything that is difficult for Him to accomplish. He is God, and because of the shed blood of Jesus Christ, we have the forgiveness of sin and great favor in God's eyes. In all the world's religions, there are hundreds of names for God, but none of them include "our Father." As God's saints, we alone have that privilege. This should give us peace in a turbulent world.

But instead of being at peace, the Church seems overcome by anxiety and fret. The Church is behaving like the waters described in Psalm 46:3: "...Its waters roar and foam..." Apprehension and dread seem to consume the Church today, causing the saints to rush off in confusion, running away headlong like a herd of stampeding cattle. We're not sure where we're going with all of our activity, but at least we're doing something. For the people who do not know God, that would be expected. But we, the blood-bought disciples of Jesus, should have a calm assurance in our world of tumult.

I believe the Church is overly anxious about spiritual warfare. It's not that I don't believe that there is a battle going on. Quite the contrary, I believe that there are fearful clashes and violent battles being waged in the heavenlies. But we need to keep perspective. These spiritual conflicts have been raging for eons. There have been skirmishes and engagements on various scales since Satan fell from heaven. Yet, through all the centuries, God has been able to handle it—without us.

We are a very self-important people when it comes to spiritual warfare. We seem to believe that ever since we woke up and realized what is going on, the whole weight of the battle is on our shoulders. Either victory or defeat will be determined by us. We will either win or lose the spiritual battles that lie ahead of us, and the outcome will be determined by our degree of vigor and militancy.

This concerned me, not because we are taking a militant stand against the enemy, however. I am disturbed because of the methods we are employing. We seem to have become engulfed in a frenzy, lacking inner peace that our God is God, and have, as a result, leaped into the fray with knowledge-deficient zeal.

Misunderstood Worship

We tend to look upon worship as one of our greatest weapons. We claim that worship is such a powerful weapon because it generates the presence of God. I've said that many times myself. We've based it on the Old Testament, where worship did indeed generate the presence of God. There we are told that God inhabits the praises of His people. But that idea must remain limited to the Old Testament. It has no place in us as New Testament believers. Because of Jesus' atoning work on the cross, God inhabits us, not just our praises.

Sometimes after a particularly great worship service

in church, we will remark that our worship brought God's presence into the church. That's not quite right. God's presence was already in the church because we were in the church, and He inhabits us. Worship just makes us more sensitive to God's presence; it doesn't bring God's presence because His presence is already there, wherever His saints are. The bottom line is that we haven't even really understood the purpose of worship.

Instead of stirring us up into a frenzy, worship should cause us to relax knowing that God is with us. This is not to say that worship has no role in spiritual warfare. The reverse is true; it has a very big role in spiritual warfare. Worship causes us to sense God's presence. Knowing that God is near gives us the assurance that God will care for us in the battle. You see, the battle is the Lord's and I think we need to be reminded of that.

Our Problem: Insecurity

Because we don't have God's peace, knowing that He is in control, we are very insecure as believers. We don't have that soothing, strengthening assurance that we are in the Lord's battle with the Lord's care. That assurance can be developed only in prayer, and we tend to avoid prayer at all costs. Without prayer we become very insecure in our relationship with God, and we have a very strong emphasis on physical action. And because we are insecure, we tend to bluster and make demands, trying to control our world. We think the only security we can have is knowing that we control the physical world. We campaign against dirty movies, abortion clinics and all sorts of other things. We are constantly struggling to control things.

Misunderstood Prayer

We have become so insecure and so militant that we have reached the point where we are trying to threaten Satan with our praying. Satan loves to get us sidetracked, getting our attention focused on fighting against him. The enemy wants us to make prayer a weapon of hype and hysteria aimed at him. But prayer is not as much a weapon as it is the means to a relationship with God. Prayer is only a threat to Satan because it develops a closeness between God and His people. In addition, prayer should never be aimed at Satan, but at God. When we focus all of our attention on God in prayer, our relationship with God grows. That relationship gives us the confidence, the certainty and the peace we need for the battle that lies before us.

With that peace and serenity, we can enter the battle. We can simply pray and leave the rest to God. This doesn't appeal to us in our insecurity. We want to run around like stampeding cattle because "at least we're doing something." But when we run around like that, we're only doing something physically, not spiritually. And it doesn't make much sense for us to "do something" physically while doing nothing spiritually when our battle is a spiritual battle. While we are on our knees and it looks like we're doing nothing in the visible world, God is active and doing much in the invisible realm.

Doctrines of Angels

We have become so insecure that we are even trying to dispatch angels for spiritual battle. We want to control angels the same way we want to control everything else. But trying to control angels is just as much of a mistake as trying to control everything else. In fact, when we try to get involved in dispatching angels, we're just meddling where we have no business being. There is not one New Testament example of believers telling angels what to do or even praying that God would dispatch angels.

Do you know what the New Testament says about dispatching angels? Matthew 4:6 says, "...He (God) will command his angels concerning you..." Matthew 13:41 states, "The Son of Man will send out his angels..." Matthew 26:53 says, "Do you think I cannot call on my Father, and He will at once put at my disposal more than twelve legions of angels?"

Angels are ministering spirits who have been sent to serve those who inherit salvation. However, the administration of angels is God's work. We are not told to command angels or even to request that God command them to do as we ask. In fact, that isn't even suggested or hinted at. The point is that we are to pray, to call to God and just learn to rest in His ability to care for us. We are to be still and know that He is God. He will answer our prayers and care for us as He sees fit. For us to call for twelve legion of angels or even twelve angels is just meddling in business that is none of our concern. God will handle that.

Consider the parable of the lost sheep. Jesus said, "See that you do not look down on (despise) one of these little ones. For I tell you that their angels in heaven always see the face of my Father in heaven," (Matthew 18:10). Jesus told his disciples not to despise those children because their angels always stand beholding the face of God. They stand with their entire attention focused on God. They get all of their direction from Him because He alone has 100 percent of their attention.

People have asked me, "Is it wrong to ask God to send angels to do certain tasks, then?" The point is it shouldn't matter to us. Our lives are to be in God's hands. God sees much more than we do. God is protecting you long before you realize you need protection. If you start to live in a self-made realm where you think you need to control the dispatching of angels and where you fight directly against Satan, then you will always be insecure. You will lack relationship with and trust in God.

I am frequently required to travel by airplane, and to this day it isn't my favorite thing to do. It's sort of unsettling. One day, as I boarded the plane, I said a quick prayer, "Lord, get me home safely." I sensed God reply, "Which home?" That did not inspire my confidence. "The home where my family lives," I answered, hoping that adequately distinguished it from my eternal home. "But you have family in both places," He said. That filled my heart with peace. Now when I board a plane, I say, "Father, I've got family in heaven, and I've got family at home. It doesn't matter to me which one I see first."

You might say, "Isn't that an uncaring attitude toward your family on earth?" It isn't in the least. The most caring thing I can do for my family is to put them entirely into God's hands. God loves my family more than I can, so why shouldn't I entrust everything to Him?

You see, we have a choice to make about how we will live. We can be the raging river described in Psalm 46:2, 3, or we can be the peaceful river of God that flows out of the throne of God. There is a river whose streams make glad the city of God, the holy place where the Most High dwells. Do you know what makes the heart of God glad? It's this river that flows out of a relationship with Him. It doesn't panic. It doesn't push. It simply flows in peace.

That peace is just a natural result of quiet, thoughtful, secluded time with your Creator. Prayer gives you a peace about God and causes you to understand that God cares more about you that you do about your own children. But because most Christians don't pray regularly, they lack this peace. They also lack a relationship with God. They may know about God, but that's not fulfilling. Knowing God, on the other hand, is fulfilling. Those who know God are content with God's ability to handle their problems. They aren't insecure, so they don't need to try to control everything around them.

Intimacy: God's Call to the Church

Isn't it interesting that while the world is convulsing in chaos and turmoil, God is calling His bride to intimacy with Him? The Psalmist writes, "Nations are in uproar, kingdoms fall..." Those words fill the headlines of our daily papers. But, in the midst of this uproar, what does God say? He says, "Be still and know that I am God. Come to Me, and I will give you rest." As we invest time in spiritual intimacy, our strength is renewed and we are able to face everything this world dishes out.

So often we try to sidestep God's call to prayer and intimacy with Him. We figure that we can renew our own strength and prepare ourselves for the battles we face in this world. We have misinterpretations of Scripture that reinforce this erroneous approach. Jesus said, "...The kingdom of heaven suffers violence, and violent men take it by force," (Matthew 11:12). We read verses like this and then go off to "take it by force" with great "violence." But Jesus wasn't advocating a bellicose spirituality, as some people claim. That "pull yourself up by your own boot-straps" mentality leads believers to put their faith in their own ability to "take it by force."

There's another problem with this interpretation of Matthew 11:12: it runs into conflict with verse 29 of the same chapter where Jesus says, "...Learn from Me, for I am gentle and humble in heart; and you shall find rest for your souls." The "take it by force" mentality usually contradicts these later words of Jesus. In our zeal to be "mighty warriors" we are disobeying the very words of Jesus. You see, our "mighty warrior" approach spawns all sorts of noise, bombast and militancy that are incom-

32

patible with the gentleness and humble heart of Jesus. (See the chapter entitled "Violent Men".)

Some have asked, "How can we take it by force if we do nothing?" It's not that we do nothing, it's that we develop a close relationship with God. That relationship becomes most powerful when it comes to demonic confrontation. I once heard the late Dr. Donald Barnhouse talk about when Jesus confronted Satan in the wilderness. The struggle Satan was having was that Jesus came to him as a man. He was defeating Satan as a man not God. Satan kept tempting Him the whole time to call on His deity to save Him, but Jesus said, "Man shall not live by bread alone."

Lucifer was created in one of the highest forms. Jesus came into this world in one of the lowest forms. Satan's pride did not like being put down by the lowly Jesus. Christ's gentleness and humility defeated Satan. This is why Satan would love for us to focus in on fighting him as long as we never develop in the same character that defeated him in the wilderness. The character of Christ in us defeats the enemy because it causes us to become the opposite of Satan. Any effort we put into fighting Satan without drawing closer to Jesus is simply laughed at by the enemy.

Let's consider what have we accomplished by "taking it by force." We smugly believe that we are enlightened concerning spiritual warfare and that we have learned how to break Satan's grip. Yet, if we really are so spiritually enriched, how is it that our world is growing worse and worse? If we know so much and our methods are so effective, why isn't there a revival sweeping across our land? Why is Satanism an ever-increasing threat to our society? I believe the reason is that we are not responding to God's call to spiritual intimacy.

That call goes beyond just praying. Many people say, "We do pray," but they still feel insecure. They still feel unable to let God run the world. They still have to be in control, ordering angels about and politically manipulating society. I believe they pray, but I also believe their motivations are amiss. They are just using prayer to obtain certain objectives. However, when you respond to God's call to spiritual intimacy, you use prayer to develop a relationship with God, and that's when you learn to trust God because you get to know Him. It's hard to trust anybody you don't know.

People who pray only to achieve certain objectives get only what they want: those objectives, and getting them does not develop a relationship. People who pray just to get things will continue to feel insecure about God because security in Him does not come through prayer: it comes through relationship. Only when you pray to develop relationship can you really be still and know that He is God.

Yet many believers today do not pray to develop a relationship with God. These people are unable to truly trust Him. For example, I know of believers who are thoroughly engrossed in crusades against abortion. I have suggested that they pray rather than picket and protest, and I have been severely criticized for making that suggestion. I have been accused of being unsympathetic toward the abortion issue, but the opposite is really true. I care very much, but I also know that the worst disservice you can do to the unborn is to place their fate in your hands rather than in God's hands. And these believers do a disservice to themselves, too, because when they pray about abortion (and I am convinced that they do), they pray only to achieve an objective, not to develop a relationship. Because they have no relationship with God, they are insecure and unable to trust Him, even though they have spent time in prayer. A relationship with God is the only thing that will allow you to be still and know that He is God. That's why many people who

34

pray prior to picketing an abortion clinic must still picket after they pray. They just can't trust God to be God and handle it, so they decide they'll handle it by picketing.

At this point, many Christians are inclined to say, "But I can't just pray! I have to do something!" But praying is doing something. That's the whole point of Psalm 46:10. God said that the only way to know that He is God—that is, beyond mere head knowledge—is by being still and doing nothing. When you do nothing, then and then only will you see that God is able to handle your problems.

Our relationship with God is what accomplishes the work of God on earth. For me to involve myself in crusading for reform in our society is fine. It's a good cause. To some extent, it will help mankind. However, it causes me to be insecure. It gets me involved in the crusade so deeply that I end up convincing myself that if I don't do it, nobody will. And I end up trying to shoulder the weight of the entire world.

One can reach a place in his relationship with God where his heart is so settled that it will baffle the world. There is a river that flows with such tranquillity that it makes the city of God glad. Tragically, many believers are not familiar with this river. They know only a raging river. They know only the stress of trying to bear all the ills of the world on their shoulders. When they pray only to reach certain objectives, they sense panic even when their prayers are answered and they reach their objectives. They become engrossed in "warfare prayer" under the impression that if they should fail to pray, Satan will capture them. Terror fills their hearts at the prospect of not praying. The problem is that they are trusting in themselves and are bearing all sorts of burdens instead of trusting God and turning their burdens over to Him. There's no being still and knowing that He is God; there's only apprehension that someday we may fail and that

Satan will then gain great victory.

Prayer: Turning Your Heart to God

Please understand that there is a very fine line involved here. The Church must pray. If the Church doesn't pray, Satan will be victorious. So far as these facts are concerned, the Church is correct, but our objectives in prayer are out of order. We need to be setting our hearts, our objectives and our directives on the heart of God.

Some people have interpreted, "Be Still" as doing nothing. They feel that I believe praying for the world is pointless. Quite the contrary is true. This does not mean we do not pray for our world. It doesn't mean we no longer interceed for people. It means that we readjust our priorities in prayer. Presently we are praying for our world because we fear we may have to change our lifestyle. We are afraid the economy is going to collapse. We are still convinced that the only priority in God's book is that of nurturing our present lifestyle.

I pray for our world because of what the sin of this world is doing to hurt our God. I pray about war in our world because of the men and women who could die without knowing Jesus. You still pray for many of the same things you are now praying for however, your motives becomes God's when you have an intimate relationship with Him. You pray for God's sake and not yours.

Consider Daniel when he prayed about the condition of Jerusalem. He prayed, "So I turned to the Lord God and pleaded with Him in prayer and petition, in fasting, and in sackcloth and ashes. I prayed to the Lord my God and confessed..." (Daniel 9:3, 4).

Daniel first turned his heart to his God. He confessed his sins and then the sins of his nation. What was the sin Daniel needed to confess? It was failure to develop relationship with God, for he said, "Just as it is written in the Law of Moses, all this disaster has come upon us, yet we have not sought the favor of the Lord our God by turning from our sins and giving attention to your truth," (Daniel 9:13).

We are rapidly approaching the fulfillment of a biblical prophesy: a time will come when men's hearts will fail them for what they see coming upon the earth. Even in light of that, we are ignoring Christ's call to intimacy. Jesus is calling His bride to His side. He wants us to know Him so that we can be still and not be afraid in the midst of the turmoil that is coming. We are misinterpreting this as a call to war, and in the process, we are engaging in prayer out of fear.

So we prepare for war (or so we think). We are studying the enemy, trying to analyze his strategies. We are even trying to figure out the names of his demons so we can bring them under the name of Jesus. We claim that we do all these things in order to break Satan's grip. But why do we want to break Satan's grip? Do we want to break Satan's grip because our hearts break over how God's heart breaks due to man's sin and separation from Him? No, we want to break Satan's grip because we don't want Satan to infringe on our pleasure-filled lifestyle. We're scared. We're insecure. We cannot be still and know that God is God. Sadly, because it is so engrossed in all this "spiritual warfare" activity, the Church isn't dealing with its own sin at all.

Real Spiritual Warfare

I think that it is tragic that the Church is so preoccupied with spiritual warfare and is so indifferent toward developing a relationship with God. But I think the tragedy is compounded by the fact that while believers are so caught up by the idea of spiritual warfare, they don't even understand what spiritual warfare is really about. They tend to believe it has something to do with giving orders to Satan, to angels and so on, in spite of the fact that there is no basis for doing any of this in God's Word.

Daniel, on the other hand, knew what spiritual warfare was all about. He went into a three-week period of prayer and fasting. That doesn't appeal to us. There's no hype, no glory and no glamour in that. But consider what happened in the spiritual realm when Daniel fasted and prayed. He engaged in one of the most powerful spiritual battles ever recorded. Daniel was up against the Prince of Persia, probably the same warring prince who still presides over Iran and Iraq, which together comprised the Persia of Daniel's day. So, how did Daniel engage the enemy? By shouting and screaming at him in the name of the Lord? By dispatching angels to engage the enemy? By proclaiming that he, Daniel, was a mighty warrior for God?

No, Daniel became the opposite of war. He became a living symbol of surrender. You see, in our battle it is our surrender to God which defeats the enemy. Consider the trouncing Moses gave to Satan in Exodus 17. When Moses kept his hands lifted, a sign of surrender, God's people won. The same thing happened with Daniel. He became humble and set his face to seek His God. The result? The Prince of Persia was stripped of his power and the angel Gabriel brought him his answer. It was the most tremendous battle recorded in the pages of Scripture, and it was followed by a tremendous revelation from the Lord.

But Daniel did it all wrong, at least according to us.

For instance, Daniel did not name the controlling spirit. Daniel did not call the angels. He didn't even address the enemy. He wasn't in the least militant, Daniel simply sought his God. And the prayers of one man broke the power of one of Satan's most powerful demons.

Today the combined efforts of the Church cannot break Satan's grip over their own community because we have chosen to fight Satan rather than exalt Christ.

The most powerful thing I can do in spiritual battle is to exalt Christ in my life. Christ is exalted in my life only as I pursue a growing relationship with Him. That relationship will cause a still, silent, but powerful river to flow through my life. That river brings pleasure to God. But without that relationship, a raging, turbulent river flows from my life. It is a river fraught with insecurity that does not bring glory to God because it indicates a lack of trust.

We are in a battle. But it is not a physical battle, it is a spiritual battle. It can only be won through our surrender. We have to be willing to trust God and surrender everything to Him, and we can only do that through an intimate relationship with Him. Only then can we be still and know that He is God. Only then can we win the battle.

THREE

THE OFFENSE OF THE CROSS

Brothers, if I am still preaching circumcision, why am I still being persecuted? In that case, the cross of Christ has been abolished.—Paul, the apostle (Gal. 5:11).

The Galatian believers to whom Paul wrote were neglecting the grace of God and the atoning work of Jesus on the cross. They were turning to a gospel of works, placing their faith in the Old Testament law, where circumcision played a prominent role. But Paul wanted nothing to do with any such false gospel. He preached only the gospel of Jesus Christ, the message of the cross. It was an offense to men, and because of that cross, Paul was persecuted.

The cross is still an offense today. Certainly to those

who are lost and refuse to accept the message of reconciliation, the cross is an offense. But it is also an offense to many believers in the Church, especially in the United States. It is an offense today for the same reason it was an offense in A.D. 57 when Paul wrote his letter: the cross of Christ means death. More specifically, it means death to our flesh, to our sinful nature.

Most people really want to avoid putting their sinful nature to death because it means putting to death the selfishness that all of us are born with. You see that selfishness in a nursery where a small child clutches a toy one of his peers wants to play with. "I want it! Mine!" the child shrieks. And unless that nature is put to death, it will reign and rule in us as adults. Many decades ago, the singer Frank Sinatra inadvertently described this nature in his song, "I Did it My Way." We all inherently want it our way. That's what got us kicked out of the garden in the first place.

But Paul, echoing the words of Jesus, preached the cross, not just in the context of Jesus' death, but in the context of practical Christian living. Paul knew that the sinful nature needed to be crucified in order for a believer to live a successful Christian life. He wrote to the Galatians, "For the sinful nature desires what is contrary to the Spirit, and the Spirit what is contrary to the sinful nature," (Galatians 5:17). Consequently, that sinful nature must be crucified. It's not just an option; it's a must.

Crossless Christianity

We live in a crossless Church. We have lost the message of self-denial. That's why so many people applaud prayer seminars, buy and read books about prayer and listen to tapes teaching about prayer, but fail to actually pray. First of all, prayer is hard work. We don't want hard work, though. We want comfort. Why engage in spiritual warfare when it is so much easier to watch television, to talk on the phone or go out socializing? The bottom line is we are selfish. We want to pursue and do the things that we think will make us happy, but we give little thought to the things that we could do that would please God. To us, the preaching of the cross is so offensive because it reminds us of how self-centered we are.

We still have high regard for the cross of Calvary, through which we enter salvation. But we are ignoring another cross. It's the cross each of us is to bear daily after we have been reconciled with God through Jesus' atoning work on His cross. Jesus didn't make it an option or something we could do for extra credit. As far as Jesus was concerned, the cross was to be an integral part of life for His followers.

> And anyone who does not take his cross and follow me is not worthy of me. Whoever finds his life will lose it, and whoever loses his life for my sake will find it (Matt. 10:38,39).

Of course, Jesus was not speaking of a literal cross. What he meant is that all of his followers were to die to self on a daily basis. Everyday we are called to die to self in order to show the world Jesus. If there is no self-denial in our lives, we are not worthy of Christ. Each day we have to be willing to do things we aren't naturally inclined to enjoy doing.

The natural response is, "That's all very nice, but do I have to do that?" or "Why do I have to do that?" We must bear our crosses, and we must do this because anything that comes to God must come through a cross of some kind. For Jesus, it was a literal cross. He had to bear His cross and endure its pain, and, since we are His disciples, we must do the same.

Please understand that self-denial will never purchase your salvation. You can deny yourself until you are blue in the face, and your self-sacrifice will not save you. Only the shed blood of Christ can bring you salvation. Nothing else can. Self-denial can't make you more saved than Christ's blood, either. Nothing can make you any more saved than the blood shed on the cross at Calvary.

However, the only way to be a true and obedient disciple of Jesus is through self-denial. In order to accomplish the work God has entrusted to us, we must die to self. When we take up our cross, we enter into God. Our life then glorifies Him.

There are two methods being used today to work for God. We can either work through the flesh or we can work through the Spirit. Most of what takes place in the name of Jesus today is accomplished through the flesh. We have singers who trust in their gifted vocal abilities to accomplish the work of God. Many preachers rely on hype, style or eloquence to accomplish the work God has given to them. These people are unwilling to work through the Spirit because that would mean dying to self.

> For we who are alive are always being given over to death for Jesus' sake so that his life may be revealed in our mortal body. So then, death is at work in us, but life is at work in you (2 Cor. 4:11,12).

Paul understood that there is only one way to show the world Jesus' life in our lives: through the death of our flesh. This is why prayer and fasting are so vital in ministry. Any minister who won't give himself over to these two exercises has very little of Jesus to offer others.

> As it is written: "For your sake, we face death all day long; we are considered as sheep to be slaughtered." No, in all these things, we are more than

conquerors through him who loved us (Rom. 8:36,37).

Paul faced death for the sake of believers. To be sure, he faced the continual threat of physical death. Zealous Jews tried to kill him on several occasions, and they were later joined by the Romans when the Empire's official policy forbade Christianity. Physical death was a daily possibility for Paul. But first he had made a decision to die to self, to die daily to his selfish desires, for then physical death was unable to instill any fear. Paul learned that only through death can we find life, that only through surrender can we find victory.

Victory in Death

Our problem is that we tend to think of victory as the absence of death, the absence of surrender. This tendency influenced the Psalmist in Psalm 44. In the first eight verses, he reflected on all the great victories God had brought to the Old Testament believers. Then in verses 9-16, the Psalmist expressed confusion because God was no longer giving them the great victories He had in the days of old. In verses 17-21, the Psalmist lamented that they had done nothing wrong, nothing deserving death or defeat.

Jesus' disciples experienced the same confusion when He spoke about the death that he would soon die. They couldn't believe that Jesus meant that He was going to literally die on a cross, and at least one of them, Simon Peter, rebuked Him. Those disciples still possessed this Old Testament mentality that assumed God would physically destroy their enemies, like the Romans who had overrun and conquered their land, and then He would establish His kingdom on earth. Jesus' followers were not yet able to see the difference between the Old Testament way of doing things and the New Testament way of doing things.

In the Old Testament, God physically destroyed the enemies of His people. But under the New Testament, the enemies of His people are destroyed through the death of His people. As we die to self, the unsaved see a greater revelation of God through us, and they are saved and are no longer our enemies. That's why Paul said that even though we face death everyday, we are more than conquerors. In the Old Testament, God's people tried to force other men to serve God. It was a physical battle between them and the will of pagans. In the New Testament, however, the battle is between God and our will. That battle can be won only through the death of self.

This is why I have always maintained that spiritual warfare is most effectively fought through the denial of self. We cannot match Satan's strength in ourselves, much less overcome him. All we have to do is become the opposite of him. For instance, because Satan is the prince of the world (John 16:11), anything we do to identify ourselves as worldly makes us powerless over Satan. Our power over the enemy comes through death to self and to the pride of this life.

> And having disarmed the powers and authorities, he made a public spectacle of them, triumphing over them by the cross (Col. 2:15).

Paul made it very clear that Jesus triumphed over Satan through the cross. To the Jews who had plotted against Him, it looked like Jesus had been defeated. The crowds who beheld Him on the cross believed that the teachers of the law had won and that He had lost. Even to His own disciples, who did not yet understand God's plan for redemption, it looked like defeat. But to the Father, it was a glorious victory because His Son could now live through the lives of His disciples, and others would see Jesus through his followers' death to self.

We have a Choice

You may feel that prayer and fasting are a waste of your time, but that's only because you do not see the development of Christ's character in your life as being important. God, however, sees it as the most important thing there is, and our will must conform to His. We must choose to bear our cross and die to self in order to develop His character within us. Jesus had to make that same decision. He could have refused to bear His cross when the appointed time came. Even after he was taken to Pilate, he could have chosen to call legions of angels to deliver him from the hands of the Jews and the Romans. He could even have come down from the cross if He had wanted. But He chose to put the Father's interests above His own personal comfort.

We, too, have a decision to make. The Father is calling us to bear a cross and to deny ourselves, and like Jesus, we can decide to refuse. We can decide to put our own interests and our own comforts before His. But Paul warned against that option.

Join with others in following my example, brothers, and take note of those who live according to the pattern we gave you. For, as I have often told you before, and now say again even with tears, many live as enemies of the cross of Christ. Their destiny is destruction, their god is their stomach, and their glory is their shame. Their mind is on earthly things. But our citizenship is in heaven. And we eagerly await a Savior from there, the Lord Jesus Christ (Phil. 3:17-20).

Paul knew that there were believers who failed to live according to the pattern he taught. They were people who made themselves enemies to the cross of Christ, but not to Christ himself. They were enemies of self-denial, individuals who refused to bear their cross. Instead they became preoccupied with enjoying all the pleasures that the world could offer them. They forgot that their citizenship was in heaven and that their greatest hope should have been the return of the Lord Jesus Christ.

> Let us fix our eyes on Jesus, the author and perfecter of our faith, who for the joy set before Him endured the cross, scorning its shame, and sat down at the right hand of God (Heb. 12:2).

We have a choice to make. We can life for pleasure and enjoyment of our flesh as enemies of the cross of Christ. Then one day when we have to give an account of our lives, we will have little or nothing to offer to God.

On the other hand, we can fix our eyes on Jesus and live as He did, dying to self and bearing our cross. If we live for God and not for ourselves, we can look with great joy and hope to the return of our Master. Then when He reviews His record of accounts and sees how wisely we invested in the kingdom while on earth, He will be pleased. He will commend us and say, "Well done, good and faithful servant."

We all have a choice to make: what are we going to do with the cross?

FOUR

THE SPIRIT OF HARLOTRY

Sin is essentially a departure from God.
—Martin Luther

God uses many things and experiences that are common to us in order to teach us about Him and about our relationship with Him. He did this throughout the Old Testament, and Jesus continued in this pattern as He taught in parables. Frequently God used marriage as an object lesson for His people, and with good reason. So much of marriage mirrors our relationship with Him.

For example, many men don't like to admit it, but it is true nonetheless: in marriage, the woman controls the level of intimacy. Men never control it. It is true that men tend to prod and pursue it, but the final decision is the woman's. This is analogous to Christ's relationship with

His bride, the Church. Jesus, the husband, never determines the degree of intimacy He will have with the Church. Like any husband, He hints and prods at intimacy, but the final decision is always the prerogative of the Church.

> The wife does not have authority over her own body, but the husband does; and likewise, the husband does not have authority over his own body, but the wife does. Stop depriving one another, except by agreement for a time that you may devote yourselves to prayer (1 Cor. 7:4,5).

These are rather well-known verses, especially to men who are trying to persuade their wives to strive for a greater degree of intimacy. However, very few believers are stretching beyond that narrow scope with these verses. As we, the Bride of Christ, apply this verse to our relationship with our Husband, the greatest dimensions of these verses are revealed. We are confronted with the sobering truth that the Church has been denying Jesus His right to us. Jesus currently has a bride that refuses Him. We simply do not desire intimacy with Him. As a result, we do not pray.

Understanding God's Heart

> When the Lord first spoke through Hosea, the Lord said to Hosea, "Go take yourself a wife of harlotry, and have children of harlotry; for the land commits flagrant harlotry, forsaking the Lord (Hos. 1:2).

In the book of Hosea, God instructed the prophet to marry Gomer, a prostitute. Hosea became a living object lesson to the people of Israel. He married a wife that he knew was going to leave him. Through his grief, the people of the land were to gain an understanding of God's grief caused by the harlotry of His people. Our lack of prayer is seen by God as His bride playing the harlot. Today's prayerless Church is "Gomer".

> So my people are bent on turning from Me. Though they (prophets) call them to the One on high, none at all exalts Him. How can I give you up, O Ephraim? How can I surrender you, O Israel? How can I make you like Admah? How can I treat you like Zeboiim? My heart is turned over within Me, all my compassions are kindled (Hos. 11:7,8).

Their own spirit of harlotry prevented them from experiencing intimacy with God, for it says, "...They do not know the Lord." Today the situation is largely the same. There is a great spiritual battle taking place between the spirit of harlotry (or lust) and the spirit of prayer (or intimacy). The spirit of harlotry is drawing us away from God. It is a self-seeking attitude, while the spirit of prayer is a selfless one. When we are enticed by our own lusts and yield to this spirit of harlotry, we lose interest in others. Instead, we are preoccupied by our own desires and all the things we want for ourselves.

> What is the source of quarrels and conflicts among you? Is not the source your pleasures (lusts) that wage war within your members? You lust and do not have; so you commit murder. And you are envious and cannot obtain; so you fight and quarrel. You do not have because you do not ask. You ask and do not receive, because you ask with wrong motives, so that you spend it on your pleasures. You adulteresses, do you not know that friendship with the world is hostility toward

God? Therefore, whoever wishes to be a friend of the world makes himself an enemy of God (James 4:1-4).

I am not totally convinced that we believe what James said in verse 4 when he said, "friendship with the world is hostility toward God." For the last couple of decades the church in America has enjoyed what the Christian lifestyle has offered them. We have been able to be Christians without anybody knowing it. We can walk through a shopping mall and nobody knows we are saved. We dress the same as the world, we do all the same activities as the world. It's been easy to hide our relationship with Christ. However, that is all coming to an end. God is calling us to a new level of commitment.

What if God suddenly made it obvious to the world that we are Christians? The question must then be asked, "Could we be Christians if it were suddenly obvious to everybody around us?" The point is that the world around us is getting so obviously non-christian that God is calling His bride to abstain from her former worldly pursuits. To refuse to do so will make us an enemy of God.

It is not uncommon today to find our "Christian" young people sitting in the local bars on weekend nights. They are not there to drink alcohol but, rather, lime water. But why drink lime water? Why not drink milk in the bar? Milk would give us away. It would become obvious that we do not belong in the bar, however, lime water gives the appearance of alcohol. Lime water allows us to sit with the ungodly and nobody will ever know we are not one of them. Or are we?

If anyone comes to you and does not bring this teaching do not receive him into your house and do not give him a greeting. For the one who gives him a greeting participates in his evil deeds (2

John 1:10,11).

The thought of giving a greeting or saying, "God bless you," or "Godspeed," was in essence announcing your blessing on them. The Scripture said if someone comes to you with a message that is contrary to the gospel of Jesus Christ, we should not give them a greeting or announce our blessing on them. Because they need to know that you are in opposition to anything that does not reflect Jesus Christ.

To show your approval of their message means you then participate in their evil deeds. In other words, we Christians are guilty by association. We cannot innocently be a part of something that does not present the gospel of Jesus Christ. There is no non-committal approach to our activities. They either glorify Christ or they do not.

I think the Church needs to re-evaluate her involvement in worldly activities. Our very presence is our announcement that we believe God would bless it. Would God bless anything that is contrary to the gospel of Jesus Christ?

God is calling us to a new level of commitment. But the spirit of harlotry is making it difficult for us to give ourselves to Him. The Church's current love affair with the world will not allow us to return to our God.

There is a great spiritual blindness in the Church today. We cannot see our need to pray. We acknowledge the need for prayer but cannot bring ourselves to it. I believe God has removed our ability to draw close to Him because we will not renounce our love for the world. The only way to remove the blindness is to repent of our attraction to the world and give ourselves totally to God. God will not allow us to be intimate with Him while we pursue the world. The spirit of harlotry is hindering the spirit of prayer.

53

Materialism and Sensuality

For all that is in the world, the lust of the eyes and
the boastful pride of life, is not from the Father but
is from the world (1 John 2:16).

When we consider the bride of Christ, we find it is
made up of both men and women. Each have a particular
area of lust. Women seem to be drawn to the things that
cover their flesh, materialism (the lust of the eyes). Men
seem to be drawn to those things which satisfy their flesh,
sensuality (the lust of the flesh). I believe men have been
given a bad deal. They certainly have problems with lust,
but I do not believe that they are any greater than the
problems women have with lust.

If a woman wants to understand how a man feels
about sex (the lust of the flesh), she must compare it to her
desire to go shopping (lust of the eyes). Ladies, does the
phrase, "shop 'til you drop" mean anything to you? I
could never figure out how a woman could get any
pleasure out of window shopping until I compared the
lust of the eyes to my desire to fulfill the flesh. Most
women cannot understand what kind of pleasure a man
can get out of looking at pornography until they compare
the lust of the flesh to their own lust of the eyes.

A glance back at Hosea's wife, Gomer, demonstrates
this point.

For their mother (Gomer) has played the harlot;
she who conceived them has acted shamefully.
For she said, "I will go after my lovers, who give
me my bread and my water, my wool and flax, my
oil and my drink," (Hos. 2:5).

Gomer did not pursue her lovers because of her great
sexual lust, but because of her material lust. She wanted

wool and flax, oil and drink.

Consider how the bride of Christ has responded to the popular faith message, with its primary focus on getting things from God. We, like Gomer, have been enticed by our own material lusts. It is very typical for the bride to be attracted to that which makes her attractive.

The practice of either the lust of the flesh or the lust of the eyes engulfs us in the pride of life. Suddenly, this life means more to us than our relationship with Christ. Suddenly a man will throw away his relationship with his wife and with Christ so that he can have an affair.

The Church today is very much wrapped up with the pride of life. This is evident by its unwillingness to give up this life to seek the life of Christ. We will not pray. We cannot give ourselves to Christ because that would mean death to the life we now live. Hosea 5:4 said our deeds will not allow us to return to God. Verse 5 tells us why: "The pride of Israel testifies against him." The pride of life keeps us from prayer. It keeps us enmeshed in our own lusts.

The only thing that will bring our homes into the relationship God desires us to have, is for the Church to go back to prayer. Our return to prayer will restore the spirit of intimacy and break the spirit of harlotry that controls our nation. However, the only thing that will bring the Church back to prayer is a spirit of repentance. The problem with repentance is that it is difficult. It hurts. Genesis 3:16 says, "...In pain you will bring forth children..." Our repentance must crush our spirit to the same extent that our sin has crushed God's Spirit.

FIVE

CHILDREN OF HARLOTRY

The best ways, the oldest ways, the ways of holiness, are the ways most quickly abandoned with
the least amount of thought.
—Charles Wesley

The year was roughly 770 B.C. God's people had
turned their backs on their Creator, who had led them out
of the bondage and misery they had known in Egypt.
They rejected intimacy with God so that they could
indulge in intimacy with the corrupt pagan world. Yet
God continued to send His prophets to them to warn
them of the wrath that was sure to come if they did not
repent and turn back to Him. Hosea was one of these
prophets who was to be a sign to the children of Israel.

God commanded Hosea to marry Gomer, a prostitute, as a sign of how He (God), was married to a prostitute, His rebellious people (Hosea 1:2). Gomer ended up going back to her lovers after she was married to Hosea. She was a woman consumed with self-preoccupation. She was a sign to God's people in 770 B.C. She is a sign to God's people today. But today, like thousands of years ago, God's people are not responding to the sign of Gomer. God's people can't see the similarities between themselves and Gomer.

We are a Church preoccupied with self. We are most concerned with enjoying ourselves and experiencing more and more pleasure. Our interests are no longer God's interests, but worldly interests. Any church that has its mind on earthly things rather than on God is actually more of a hindrance to Him than a help. Because of our harlotry with the world we are birthing children of harlotry into the Church (Hosea 1:2). Because they have been birthed into a worldly church, many of today's converts are easily distracted by the world.

The Devil's Workshop

From that time, Jesus Christ began to show His disciples that He must go to Jerusalem, and suffer many things from the elders and chief priests and scribes, and be killed, and be raised up on the third day. And Peter took Him aside and began to rebuke Him, "God forbid it, Lord! This shall never happen to you." But He turned to Peter and said to Peter, "Get behind Me, Satan! You are a stumbling block to Me; for you are not setting your mind on God's interests, but man's," (Matt. 16:21-23).

When Jesus began to predict His death and resurrection, Satan used Peter's love for the world to influence him. Peter loved his life as a disciple of Jesus. It was exciting. It was wondrous. It was so unlike the religious system of the day. It looked like Jesus was going to clean up and perfect that religious system. What's more, he knew Jesus was the Messiah, and, like all Jews, Peter expected the Messiah to overthrow the Roman Empire and establish the throne of David in Jerusalem again. He had his eyes on the world and on what pleased him. He did not see God's plan of redemption. He did not see the death of Christ for the victory it would be. As a result, he became a stumbling block.

Jesus knew the Father's plan, and He knew it was not what Peter envisioned. Jesus didn't want to save the religious system of the day. It had to die so that it could be resurrected with newness of life.

Similarly our Church today must die. It must die to self so that it can reach a lost world. Only through repentance will we change the world. Our pursuit of God is the only thing that will make a difference for eternity. Political lobbying, popular in many of our churches, won't bring people to a saving knowledge of Jesus Christ. We will not bring about moral change through legislation. We must seek God first; first before our pleasure, first before our attempts to minister to the world.

As it is, the world isn't terribly impressed by us. The world has seen a great deal of sin in our camp. We have been telling them that Jesus can make their homes happy, while our ministers are running off with their secretaries. We have told them that Jesus will tame their rebellious young people, while our kids drink, dance and rock 'n' roll, all in the name of Jesus. We have told the world that Jesus can supply all their needs, while our preachers/evangelists are begging and pleading for more money. We have said, "Jesus can set you free," while we burn with lust. In all these statements and more, we have emphasized the benefits of the resurrection while completely ignoring the Lordship of Christ. Whatever happened to the Lordship of Christ? It was discarded when we began to pursue things from Jesus rather than Jesus Himself.

For the most part, the Church in America is a harlot Church because it will not seek God through prayer. Instead it pursues the pleasures of this world. Jesus does not want His Church to continue in its present condition. She must die in order to be resurrected with newness of life.

Seeking God

I find it interesting that today's Church focuses so heavily on reforming our society. We seek laws and judicial rulings to improve the moral climate of our nation. Yet, as Christ's bride, we are seldom even moderately interested in pursuing Him. Instead we concentrate on rehabilitating our sinful world. One of the reasons believers give for this preoccupation is that it safeguards our religious freedom. There's a subtlety in that reason that's easy to miss: our religious freedom represents our lifestyle, not a relationship. The fact is we seem to be far more concerned with our lifestyle than we are about Jesus. Our primary pursuit in life should be developing an intimate relationship with Jesus, but He is not the first concern of our Church. If He were, our land would be automatically healed.

> If my people who are called by My name will humble themselves and pray, and seek My face and turn from their wicked ways, then I will hear from heaven, will forgive their sin, and will heal their land (2 Chron. 7:14).

This verse is often misunderstood. I have heard many

lay people and ministers quote this verse, then proceed to explain that it means we need to pray for our sinful nation. But nowhere in that verse are God's people urged to pray for their nation. What the verse does urge God's people to do is humble themselves, pray, seek the face of God, and turn from their wickedness. Then God would forgive their sin. That, in turn, would heal the land. We often gather to pray for our country because we say there's something wrong with "them"—the unsaved. We are partly correct—there is something wrong with the unsaved: they need to be saved. But we also need to realize there's something wrong with us. We need to give more attention to the part of that verse that says God will forgive the Church of its sin. It is the sin of prayerlessness that keeps our land from being healed.

You see, the spiritual condition of the Church always determines the moral condition of the world. Some believers refer to rallies like Washington for Jesus, where they gathered to pray for the country and then say they were practicing 2 Chronicles 7:14. But that verse wasn't written in order to convince us to pray for our nation. It was written to provoke us to seek God's face (not His hand of blessing) because then the land is healed automatically.

There is certainly nothing wrong with praying for our nation. That is a scriptural thing to do, in fact. But God isn't as concerned about our special prayer thrusts as He is about us developing a lifestyle of prayer in which He is the primary reason we are praying. If we only pray that our land will be healed, we are failing to practice 2 Chronicles 7:14. That verse admonishes us to seek God, not just seek something from Him.

Prayer Prerequisite: Humility

Sometimes we become so engrossed in the idea of

praying for our nation so that our land will be healed, we overlook another facet of this verse: humility. We are called to humble ourselves and seek His face. I don't think this means we have to be 100% humble before we can pray (sometimes the only way God can humble us is through prayer). However, it means we must let go of some of our pride and just trust God. So often our pride drives us to "do something"; our pride tells us prayer isn't enough. Our pride convinces us that we can save our nation through our human efforts. But to do nothing but pray would be to give God control of our lives and control of our country. In order to do this, we have to humble ourselves and admit that all of our physical efforts to save our country have been futile.

Earlier I mentioned that many believers become political lobbyists because they fear that we might otherwise lose our religious freedom. But just what would happen if we lost our civil religious freedoms? I suspect it would force us to go back to diligently praying and seeking our God. That would then cause us to love all of our Christian brothers and sisters regardless of their theological stance. We would go back to sharing all of our goods with others. We would live by faith in God rather than by faith in our finances. We would probably end up as the bride of Christ without spot or wrinkle. But our eyes are so intently fixed on the pride of life that we can no longer see the real need of the Church. As a result, we are becoming the same stumbling block to Jesus that Peter was in Matthew 16.

Do you really believe God wants us to spend our time cleaning up our society through political reform? What about our own hearts? Don't they mean anything to God? As it is, our hearts have become so deceived, we believe that God is so pleased with us that his top priority is seeing to it that we can indulge our flesh, making sure we have nonstop comfort.

We have so thoroughly lost our perspective that we pour thousands of dollars into so-called ministries which are dedicated to cleaning up television in the United States. The people involved in these "ministries" spend hours "monitoring" all the filth on television in order to build a case against lewd television programming. Do you think monitoring filth is pleasing to God? Don't you think the heart of the one monitoring the filth is important to God? Some would argue that the end (i.e., cleaning up television) justifies the means (i.e., monitoring T.V.'s filth). But do you believe God is even pleased with the end, let alone the means? Does God really want us to clean up television programming? Just consider how much time "Christians" waste in front of their T.V. sets watching worldly filth, while at the same time they claim they haven't enough time to pray as they ought. How much more would they watch television if it offered more wholesome viewing? Prayer would be cast right out the window if television was morally upright.

Recently while I was thumbing through a very popular Christian magazine, I happened upon a movie review. It was the last thing I expected to find in a Christian magazine. The accompanying photograph of the movie's cast included an actress who is a self-proclaimed member of the New Age Movement. Here was a woman who claims she is God being glorified in a Christian magazine. The final synopsis concluded that it was a good movie, having a good story line. I couldn't believe that Christianity in America has degenerated so much. If a believer chooses to go see a movie, that is between him and his God. However, any medium which has such enormous potential to influence Christians as this magazine does should be more careful to avoid presenting a message that is contrary to the gospel of Jesus Christ.

We have become a harlot as a Church. The harlot is characterized as someone who is not satisfied with just one lover. The religious harlot is not satisfied with just Jesus. We demand worldly lovers, too. I remember watching a T.V. show—a Christian one— which featured a "Christian" movie critic (not a critic of Christian movies, but a critic of secular movies). He was asked why he felt it is necessary to have a movie critic for Christians. He explained that a Gallup poll had recently discovered that Christians attend movies and that they do so regardless of the movie ratings. "Since Christians are attending anyway, I thought I could save them some money by recommending the good ones."

First of all, in order to separate the good from the bad, he must review the bad as well as the good. That doesn't please God. Secondly, this "Christian" movie critic is pushing the same philosophy the world is advocating in regards to the AIDS epidemic. He's saying, "Since you're going to movies anyway, make sure you go to the good ones." The world is saying, "Since you are going to have sex outside of marriage; just be careful, and make sure it's safe sex." Whatever happened to preaching abstinence? Movies are one of many other lovers the Church has today. Who would ever think of giving them up, for Jesus' sake.

Isn't it a shame that we cannot preach holiness any more? Because we as adults do not wish to practice holiness or to preach holiness, we are bringing up children of harlotry in our churches.

Children of Harlotry

The harlot lives for nurturing the flesh. So it should come as no surprise that Christian rock music fits so comfortably into the harlot Church. It has Christian lyrics, it has Christian artists, and it has a spirit of harlotry.

The children of harlotry can be readily identified by one characteristic: they must be continuously tantalized by worldly activity. They cannot keep their eyes on Jesus alone. Their eyes wander from Jesus to the world, back to Jesus then to entertainment, back to Jesus then to social activities. It seems that we could not keep our kids in the church today if it weren't for Christian rock 'n' roll and amusement parks. I have often heard young people threaten their parents by saying, "If you won't let me have Christian rock music, then I won't go to church." They will only stay true to Jesus if they can have another lover, too. So, in essence, that isn't staying true to Jesus anyway.

Yet the Christian rock artists seem so dedicated to the things of God. That confused me. After praying about this for some time, the Lord spoke to me and said, "The harlot can have more than one lover." Finally it hit me. The harlot can be dedicated to and love Jesus Christ, but the harlot will never be satisfied with just Jesus. They must have the world also. No one can deny their profession of dedication to the things of God, but they also have a dedication to the things of the world.

The Satanic church believes that the Christian church will support the rise of Satanism within its own ranks. Our initial reaction is, "That could never be. We would never knowingly let Satan into the church." However, consider what James wrote: "You adulteresses (harlots), do you not know that friendship with the world is enmity with God? Therefore, whoever wishes to be a friend of the world makes himself an enemy of God." To make oneself an enemy of God is the ultimate expression of Satan, and consequently Satanism. God sees our involvement with the world as practicing Satanism or pursuing other gods.

Where rock music is concerned, I have observed that there is a connection between secular rock music and Satanism. As police authorities investigate crimes related to Satanism, they, too, see a connection to heavy-metal rock music. What astonishes me is that Christians cannot see any connection between Christian rock music and the worldliness of today's church kids.

Satanic Influence: Rebellion

The very spirit of rock music is rebellion, regardless of whether it's Christian or secular music. Because secular rock music is so worldly, we can safely say that it's not rebellion against the world. It sides with the world. It's actually rebellion against Jesus. And so is Christian rock music. Teen-age advocates of rock music are quick to reply, "No, it's not rebellion against Jesus. It's rebellion against this evil world." But that argument doesn't hold much water. The very nature of rebellion is to oppose or go against something. If we are really rebelling against the world, then, by definition, we cannot imitate the world. You never imitate what you are rebelling against. Yet Christian rock imitates those who worship Satan. If it were really rebellion against a corrupt world, then it would not imitate that same world. Instead, Christian rock really opposes the holy standard the Church is trying to promote.

Christian rock music has a Satanic, self-promoting spirit. Instead of promoting death to all you represented before you became a Christian, it promotes the same lifestyle you lived before you met Christ. According to the philosophy of Christian rock music, nothing has to change. The new Christian convert can still wear black T-shirts promoting the group they worship. He can still listen to the same style of music, too. What's worse, it seems to imply that he can live exactly as he did before he was saved. The question must be asked, "What are Christian rock converts converted to? If "old things" do not pass away, there has been no conversion regardless of their profession.

The worldly desire it creates is enticing our young people to imitate evil in many, many ways. Today it is not uncommon for the guys in our churches to wear an earring in one ear, just as the homosexuals do. Ungodly rock groups now set the fashion trends for our church kids. Our people, both young and old, wear hair styles that imitate those who do not know God. Why is there this flirtation with the world, this enticement to identify with the world? The answer is quite simple. It is the harlot spirit that we are breeding.

This spirit manifests itself in other ways. For example, consider premarital sex among our young people. Why do they have such a problem in this area? It's because their music caters to the flesh. Our kids claim that they are not attracted to their music by the beat, saying that they are instead attracted by the words. If what they claim is true, they should be very attracted to the church hymnal because you can't find better words than you will in there.

Worshiping God or Man?

Christian rock displays one other serious flaw: worship of itself. I hear our young people talk more about Christian rock music than they do about Jesus. They seem to know more about their favorite rock group than they do about Jesus. Their favorite musicians seem to be the center of their Christianity. The concert T-shirts that they wear exalt the names, faces, slogans and songs of these musicians.

If Jesus returned to earth in bodily form, which rock group's T-shirt would he wear? Which of his ears would be pierced for an earring? Those questions make some uncomfortable, but they are questions which we must come to grips with.

Selling admission tickets to concerts is further exaltation of self. What if Evangelists sold tickets for a revival?

That single action speaks volumes. It says, "I am worthy of you spending God's money on me." It pompously blusters, "Freely I've received, but you're going to have to pay." It says, "Not everyone is welcome; only those who can afford me are worthy of me and my performance." And this should not surprise us because it is just a symptom of a disease that afflicts the Christian recording industry. Large segments of the Christian recording industry have contracted the same disease which has infected the secular industry for decades: corruption. Money has become its god, so anyone who allows himself to be influenced by it will also partake of its evil (2 John 1:10, 11).

Converted Into What?

Again I will say that I don't doubt the sincerity of Christian artists who play and sing this subtle form of Satanism. However, I do believe they are sincerely deceived if they believe that what they are promoting is developing the character of Christ in their followers. What they promote has very little to do with Jesus, and so their cheering fans see very little of Jesus. What they see is a musical performance, and that becomes the center of Christianity to them. They grow to thrive on that and depend on that instead of thriving and depending on Jesus. Only a harlot spirit develops a dependency on something other than Christ.

I am aware that these performers defend their style of music and dress by pointing at all the converts they've won. But we must keep in mind that like produces like. Worldliness breeds worldliness. When we use a worldly means to promote the gospel, we give birth to converts who love the world. If we draw them to Christ through worldly means, then it is the world which nurtures them. Inevitably, because they love the world, they become an

68

enemy of God (James 4:4). Those are not the kind of converts the Church needs. The Church today needs single-minded people who will sell out to Jesus and serve Him, even if it costs them comfort in this life.

Instead of bringing people to Christ, we are bringing Christ to people. We are no longer saying, "Come to Jesus. Here is what He represents, including His Lordship over us." Instead we are saying, "Here is Jesus. He will become anything you already are. There is no need for you to change anything in your life. Just come and get your sins washed away." We don't tell them that they will have to give up their other gods and other lovers. We pass on to them the harlot spirit which says, "I'll become a lover of Christ as long as I have my other lovers."

Christian Music Is Not All Bad

Let me clarify something here. I do not believe that all contemporary Christian music falls into the category of harlotry. There are still groups and musicians that emulate the presence of God, but they are few and far between. Why? Because to get that touch of God on your ministry, you have to spend time with Him.

What I'm talking about transcends a quick supplication offered before a concert. I would suspect a great many Christian artists do that much. However, there are few who dare to linger in God's presence daily and at times when they're not about to perform. There are few who make seeking God the primary goal of their lives. This becomes evident by the startling number of Christian performers who are so willing to take the glory from Jesus and heap it upon themselves.

I charge the gospel artists today to go back to the free gospel, to go back to concerts in the church, to go back to a life of faith, to go back to singing about Jesus and His shed blood. There's not much glitz or glory for man in what I am suggesting, so I realize the chances of it happening are quite slim indeed. Sadly, what we call a love for God today is often just a love for money, and our commitment to God depends on the size of the crowd.

I have neither the time nor the desire to go through a list of Christian musicians to try to decide who is good and who isn't. First of all, that's not my place. Secondly, nobody needs for me to do that because the fruit of their music will determine the validity of their ministry. You'll be able to tell what their music is worth by the commitment of their converts.

We must be very careful as we attempt to be ministers for God. Peter tried to help Jesus out, but became a tool of Satan because he failed to see things as God saw them. Our feeble efforts to help God out by altering the message of self-denial that is inherent in the true gospel has caused many to become instruments of Satan, children of harlotry.

SIX

ISAAC VS. ISHMAEL

My ways are not your ways, neither are My
thoughts your thoughts.
—God (Isa. 55:8)

After these things the word of the Lord came to
Abram in a vision, saying, "Do not fear Abram, I am a
shield to you; your reward shall be very great." And
Abram said, "O Lord God, what wilt Thou give me, since
I am childless, and the heir of my house is Eliezer of
Damascus? Since Thou hast given no offspring to me, one
born in my house is my heir." Then behold, the word of
the Lord came to him saying, "This man will not be your
heir, but one who shall come forth from your own body,
he shall be your heir." And He took him outside and said,
"Now look toward the heavens, and count the stars, if you
are able to count them." And He said to him, "So shall
your descendants be," (Genesis 15:1-5). Abram listens to

the voice of God.

Abram was a very wealthy man with a very big problem: he had no son to inherit his wealth. His wife was too old to have children, so there seemed to be little hope for him. But then God intervened and promised to solve Abram's problem. He promised that He would give Abram not just a son, but a multitude of descendants. That would be a miracle indeed. No one even believed Abram would have so much as a single son, let alone thousands upon thousands of descendants. Yet, that was God's plan. He planned to confound the wisdom of man and to manifest His own glory and power.

But after months passed, and his wife, Sarai, seemed no closer to giving birth than she ever had, doubt entered the picture. God's promise no longer seemed adequate, so man decided that he would help things along. Man was unable to patiently wait for his faithful God to respond, so he set about doing this his way.

> So Sarai said to Abram, 'Now behold, the Lord has prevented me from bearing children. Please go in to my maid; perhaps I shall obtain children through her.' And Abram listened to the voice of Sarai (Gen. 16:2).

Abram now listens to the voice of man, giving more heed to it than to the words God had spoken to him earlier. Like all the men around him, he, too, began to think the words God had spoken were folly. How could his wife give birth to a child when she was ninety years old? Perhaps God's promise was true, he figured, but surely it could not be fulfilled through his wife, Sarai; there must have been some other way to make it come true, he thought. So Abram went off and did things the way he thought they should have been done instead of the way God said they should have been done.

Because Abram did things his way instead of God's, he failed to receive the promise through his efforts. The son (Ishmael) he received through his wife's servant was not the offspring he had hoped for. An angel of the Lord came and said, "And he will be a wild donkey of a man. His hand will be against everyone, and everyone's hand will be against him; and he will live to the east of all his brothers," (Genesis 16:12). That wasn't what Abram had expected: it wasn't what he wanted. Ishmael was a continual problem for his father, Abram. But that's what always happens when the voice of man supersedes the voice of God: we have problems. Ishmael was a problem for Abram, and he is a problem for us today.

> And you, brethren, like Isaac, are children of promise. But at that time he who was born according to the flesh persecuted him who was born according to the Spirit, so it is now also (Gal. 4:28).

There are those who are born of the Spirit into the Kingdom of God. They are born through God's means. Then there are those who are born into the Kingdom of God who have come in through fleshly means. They have been enticed through ways we have learned to attract people to the Church. Right now we are finding that people who are born into the Kingdom of God through fleshly means, rather than through the Spirit, will rise up and remain a continual problem for the people of the spirit. They will have a contrary spirit. They will want to do God's work through the flesh, through talent, through clever advertising and so on. Those born of the Spirit, however, will not do things that way. They will depend on prayer and on the Holy Spirit to do God's work. This creates conflict and stress.

The reason we have this problem is that we feel confident that we know God's will, so we immediately rush off to accomplish that will. But many times we know God's will without understanding His timing. We fail to realize that knowing God's will isn't the same as understanding God's timing and God's methods. Like Abram, we go off and try to accomplish God's will our way, and we end up being very disappointed with the results of our labors because they aren't what we thought God wanted.

> My ways are not your ways, neither are my thoughts your thoughts (Isa. 55:8).

We need to understand God's will when it comes to building God's kingdom, but, like Abram, we need to know more than that. We also need to know the ways of God and the timing of God. A thorough knowledge of one or even two of these items is not sufficient for doing God's work. We need all three.

Understanding the Will of God

Interestingly enough, of these three factors, the will of God, the ways of God, and the timing of God, the will of God is the easiest to determine when it comes to the work of the Church. God's will for the Church has been very clearly and precisely explained in His written Word. For example, we know that it is God's will that all men should be saved.

> God is not slack concerning his promise, as some men count slackness, but is longsuffering toward us not willing that any should perish, but that all men should come to repentance (2 Peter 3:9).

Because this is so clearly explained in God's Word, we don't have to wonder whether or not we should share the message of salvation with someone. We should never ask

God whether or not he wants us to witness to someone because His Word has already told us that it is His will that we spread the good news of redemption. The questions we should ask are "When is the right time to share?" and "What are the right methods of sharing?"

As soon as I was certain that God had called me to a prayer ministry, I realized that, like salvation, God's call to prayer was for everyone. I knew it was God's will for me to take the message of prayer to any Church that would listen to it. If a Church calls me and asks if I would conduct a prayer seminar for them, I don't first ask God if it is His will for me to do so. I already know it is. That's the easy part. What I pray about is timing. When would God want me to do it?

God's Timing

Our tendency is to act upon a promise rather than to wait for its fulfillment. That was the sin of Abram. He knew God had promised him a son, so he decided to make that promise come true through his own efforts, rather than waiting for the fulfillment of the promise. From Abram's experience, we learn that mere man cannot force the fulfillment of God's will.

> But when the fulness of the time came, God sent forth His Son, born of a woman, born under the Law (Gal. 4:4).

God works in the fulness of time, when all things have been set in order. Only God really knows when all things have been set in order because only God has a knowledge of all things. He is the only one who sees the big picture. Man is only able to see a few pieces of that picture at a time, so it is crucial that he gives ear to his God. For the Lord alone is omniscient, and He alone will know when the time for any given thing is right.

When my ministry was just in its infancy, God gave me a promise. I was having lunch with a couple who attended a church where I had just finished ministering. After we finished eating lunch, they invited me to join them for a time of communion. I thought that was a little odd. It was probably the first time I had ever been given such a spontaneous and unexpected invitation to share communion, but since we were in their home, it seemed appropriate. During our time together, God began to minister through her with a word of prophecy. She said she saw me writing at a desk and that Jesus had His hand on me. Then she said, "What I saw you writing would be in demand across our country."

Pray-Tell Ministries was only a few months old when that word of prophecy was given. I didn't have any material that I could make into a magazine article, let alone enough material to write a book. I told an elderly Christian woman about this prophecy because I valued her insight after her many years of faithfulness to God. She said, "Tuck it away, Ron. If it is really a word of prophecy from God it will come to pass. If it isn't from God, forget about it. One thing is sure, you cannot force the fulfillment of it." Three years later I was doing a seminar in Iowa when I happened to go with the pastor to visit a lady at the hospital. During that visit, I met the lady's brother, Cliff Dudley, the man who later became my publisher. He asked me all sorts of questions about what I was doing in my ministry. Usually people don't ask me many questions after they hear I have a prayer ministry for fear they'll find out too much and have to start praying.

But that night Cliff called me to ask if I would have breakfast with him the next morning. I agreed and met with him the next day. After eating and sharing for awhile, Cliff told me that when I walked into the hospital room, God told him he should publish my book. He then asked, "Do you have a book?" It was amazing. I had written a prayer seminar which I felt that God wanted me to publish, but I didn't know anything about writing or publishing books, so I prayed about it and left the matter to God because it was beyond my knowledge or experience. When I explained this to Cliff, he quickly replied, "I know exactly what needs to be done. I own New Leaf Press." (A Christian Publishing House). What resulted was the publication of my first book, *Prayer Can Change Your Marriage,* as well as others.

We cannot force the fulfillment of God's promises. We can force an end result, but that's not fulfillment. Abram tried to force the fulfillment of God's promise to him, but he ended up with Ishmael, and Ishmael was not the fulfillment of God's promise to Abram. Abram succeeded in getting a son, but failed to receive God's promise through that son. Timing is crucial.

Therefore, the Lord longs to be gracious to you, and therefore He waits on high to have compassion on you. For the Lord is a God of justice; how blessed are all those who long for Him (Isa. 30:18).

According to this verse, God has an intense desire to be gracious to us, for it says that He "longs" to do so. But it also says that He waits. Why would he wait if he longs to do something? There are times when God waits so that He can teach us to wait. Waiting deals with timing, so again we see the importance of timing.

But you might ask, "Why does God want to teach us to wait?" He teaches us to wait so that He will be exalted through our actions. When we wait until God's time is right, God is exalted. When Isaac was born, God was exalted because that was the right time for Him to carry out his promise. But when Abram impatiently did things

77

according to his earthly time schedule, ignoring God's heavenly time schedule, God was not glorified.

We also need to realize the difference between God's schedule and ours. A day to the Lord is a thousand years to us, so when God says, "Wait a minute," that "minute" could last for years. Most theologians believe Abram did not see God's promise fulfilled for at least twenty-five years after God made that promise. When God called Moses to the top of the mountain to give him the Law, do you know what God said? He said, "Come to the top of the mountain and be there." Be there! Don't do anything else, just be there. Moses listened to God, went to the top and waited. He waited seven days before God said a word to him. After that, he received one of the greatest revelations ever given to man: the Ten Commandments. Before Moses went up, however, he told Aaron and the others to wait, but they gave up after a short time and decided to do something on their own. The man of the spirit knows how to wait on God. The people of the flesh struggle with this.

Have you ever been stuck in traffic and found yourself waiting against your will? Maybe you were waiting for a train to pass at a railroad crossing. Suddenly you decided you had waited long enough and so you darted down a side road. It may not have been the right thing to do, it may have even taken longer to reach your destination than if you had waited, but at least you were moving again. Refusing to wait for traffic may not be such a big deal, but refusing to wait for God is a very big deal.

Moses told Aaron to wait, but Aaron and the people decided not to. They said, "We've waited long enough. Moses may never come back." Just like us, they were overcome by a desire to do something, even if it wasn't the right thing. They figured, "At least it's better than doing nothing." It wasn't better than doing nothing, though, for they made an idol, a golden calf. That's just what we do when we refuse to wait for God. When we move out of God's timing, then that which we do in the name of God becomes an idol.

The Ways of God

Referring back to Isaiah 30, we find that after verse 18 tells us that God is teaching us to wait, verse 21 tells us that once we learn to wait for God's timing, we will then learn the ways of God.

And your ears will hear a word behind you, "This is the way, walk in it," whenever you turn to the right or to the left (Isa. 30:21).

God will give us direction, telling us which way to go. When we walk in God's way, we walk in the Spirit. As we walk in the Spirit, God builds the Church the way he wants it to be. But when we fail to walk in God's ways, as the Church today tends to do, we walk in the flesh. The result is that we build the Church, shaping it into what we want it to be. Subsequently, we give birth to Ishmael rather than Isaac. When God does build the Church we develop dependency upon the work of our hands. That's what happened in Moses' day. Aaron and the people did not wait for God, so they began to trust the work of their own hands.

The Work of Thy Hands

Their land has also been filled with idols; they worship the work of their hands, that which their fingers have made (Isa. 2:8).

Throughout the book of Isaiah, we see God's people being rebuked because they worshipped the work of their own hands. They worshipped idols made of silver, gold, stone and even wood. They were finely crafted works, too, the apex of their artistic abilities. That's what the people worshipped, and that is the natural consequence of not waiting for God's perfect timing.

Description of an Idol

Their idols are silver and gold, the work of man's hands. They have mouths, but they cannot speak; they have eyes, but they cannot see; they have ears, but they cannot hear; they have noses, but they cannot smell; they have hands, but they cannot feel, they have feet, but they cannot walk; they cannot make a sound with their throat. Those who make them will become like them, everyone who trusts in them (Psa. 115:4-8).

If the Church of Jesus Christ does things man's way, if we listen to the voice of man and the voice of human logic, then we will begin to build idols rather than the true Church. Even today there are many Ishmael churches. The Ishmael church is just like the idol. It will no longer speak for God. It will lose its spiritual sight. It will lose its spiritual hearing. It will lose its spiritual discernment. It will lose its spiritual sensitivity. It will no longer walk the path of God.

By far the most devastating thing about the Ishmael (idol) church is what verse 8 said in the preceding verses. "Those who make them will become like them" Not only does the Church itself no longer have the life of God in it, but neither do those who started it. Those who make idols become like idols.

Consider how much of "God's work" is being done without prayer. That's worshipping the work of our own hands. So many times, Churches will plan outreaches to the community without basing them on prayer. Instead, they sit down and brainstorm: What would be most appealing to people? What would be the most fun? What would be the least offensive? What would be the least "Churchy?" What would be most entertaining? Then they set out to build with their own hands an outreach that responds favorably to all these criteria. That outreach then becomes an idol. Not only will we become like that idol we build, but so will our converts.

Then he answered and said to me, "This is the word of the Lord to Zerubbabel saying, Not by might nor by power, but by my Spirit, says the Lord of hosts (Zech. 4:6).

If we are going to reach our world with the gospel, we cannot depend upon what man can do. We mustn't sit and ask, "What will draw people to this outreach?" We should already know that nothing can draw people like the Holy Spirit can. Our might and power do not impress God. No matter how sophisticated our outreach is, it will not impress God unless we rely on the Holy Spirit.

We cannot conduct spiritual business through a church which depends on works of the flesh. Outreaches that are built on the flesh may draw people, and some people may indeed accept Jesus, but we will lose interest in spiritual business as a church. We will tend to become more interested in our own desires rather than God's.

For they all seek after their own interests, not those of Christ Jesus (Phil. 2:21).

Paul said Timothy was one of the few who truly wanted what God wanted, rather than what appealed to his flesh. Timothy wanted his God glorified more than himself. Can you imagine that? God's Church in the United States is ensnared in a lust for success. Our drive

81

for success has replaced our desire to know God and to glorify Him. Instead, we want men to regard us saints as successful. To be found successful we try to force the the hand of God. For instance, we reason that a successful church is a church with a large congregation, so we strive for big churches. There is nothing wrong with a big church. Consider the New Testament Church. But what are we doing to draw people? The New Testament Church grew because it drew people through miracles and the manifest power of God. But we don't want to pray and wait on God, so we do things our way. We consult successful businessmen and use their principles for success, then whitewash them with Scripture to make them seem spiritual. We are ending up with many more Ishmael churches than we are Isaac churches. We want to do things our way, the human fleshly way. Consequently, marketing is fast replacing miracles.

Our interests in our churches are having less and less to do with God's interests. We are beginning to see in our Pentecostal churches the same thing I saw in the main line church I was saved out of: A spirit of repentance has been replaced by a spirit of enlistment. The primary concern in too many of our churches is filling the church building. Our unspoken message is, "Get 'em in at any cost. Don't convict and convert - enlist and enjoy."

The end result is that our churches are filled with Ishmaels. They look very much like the idols we created to attract them to our "fun" churches: they're spiritually unenlightened and always causing conflicts. They cannot take on the believer's mind.

The Elite

A friend of mine, a pastor, told me about a spirituality elite group of pastors he heard about while attending a ministers' conference. He and his wife met another pastor and his wife, and ended up discussing the ministry, even though they had previously never met. This minister told my friend about an exclusive group of pastors who met to exchange ideas about ways to cause their churches to grow more numerically. Only ministers who pastored churches with congregations totaling 1,000 or more were invited. In fact, this meeting was so exclusive that very few people even knew about it. Attendance was by invitation only. My friend said he was disturbed by any group in the Church which regarded itself as elite, exalting itself above others. I am even more concerned that it is pastors who are leading this call to elitism.

I am sad to say that this elitist attitude is prevalent among many ministers today. It is this spirit that fuels the spirit of enlistment. If, through enlistment, you can get enough people in your church, you can become one of the "elite," a group that is "obviously blessed by God." How could God's blessing rest upon any church with a congregation of less than 1,000 people? I would note, however, a pastor who has a church of 5,000 stated that "...Probably half of my people understand Christianity." I can't help but wonder how half of them could fail to understand Christianity if they were attending a church that preaches the gospel!

Do you see the pressure this pastor faces? If he starts preaching the true gospel of repentance, he will stand to lose at least half of his congregation who will be unhappy that their cotton-candy Christianity is being taken from them. He would be left only with the remnant who would be willing to receive his message. How could he take that change in this elitist age? Presently he is considered a success because of the size of his Church. He gets to go to all the "elite" meetings. In fact, he is often the speaker. He's the one that "God" has chosen to show these other pastors how to do it. If he lost half of his congregation or more due to righteous preaching, his elitist friends would inform him that "God" unchose him, and they could even ask him to leave.

If that man really began preaching a gospel with repentance in it and half of his people left, he would be condemned by man as a failure. God forbid that we would consider a man a success due to the spirituality of his Church. Certainly numbers must be more important. Some of the most spiritual Churches I have ever held seminars in were very small in comparison. Right now we are saying, "success at any cost."

The rational for enlistment is that once you get them in the Church, they will hear the true message, convert and be saved. But these saints get so obsessed with getting people into their Church that they forget about the true message. They concentrate on fun, entertainment and a non-offensive ambiance. Then when they finally get all these people into their Church, they are afraid to "offend" them with the true message of the gospel (which includes repentance), so those people from outside seldom (if ever) hear that message. Consequently, they never changed.

The enlistment philosophy is incompatible with the gospel of holiness and repentance. Enlistment advocates getting people into the Church, then turning them from the world. But repentance calls for people to turn from the world before they get into Church. Because they are incompatible, if you change from one philosophy to another, you're going to lose people. If the congregation is used to attending an enlistment Church, most will probably want nothing to do with repentance.

Not all pastors, however, measure the value of their ministries by this so-called "success". Pastor Dave Robinson has a very exceptional philosophy of ministry. He has an inner-city Church in the heart of Chicago. Seventy-five percent of his people are involved in an accountable ministry. His philosophy is that if you are going to come to his Church, you are going to work for God. He told me that he realizes he will never experience phenomenal growth because of his message. His message is repentance. Then he tells his congregation that if they wish to call themselves Christians, they had better do something for God or get out. You can't be an idle Christian; it's a contradiction in terms.

Don't be mislead, this is no small work. They have a ministry that is touching the inner city of Chicago. They have hundreds of people working their mission field. It is a fountain-head Church. And, it is a Church which preaches repentance.

Spiritual Intercession

The problem as I see it is that through the lack of prayer, which results in relying on man's abilities to do God's work, many of today's converts never take on the mind of Christ.

Have this attitude in yourselves which was also in Christ Jesus (Phil. 2:5).

New believers don't seem to really grasp what new life in Christ really means. They have a hard time equating being born-again with changing their lifestyle. They can't believe that they should change anything in their lives. But then how could anyone won to Christ through Christian rock music ever grasp the fact that they are to turn from worldliness? If those who lead people to Christ have not turned from their worldliness, neither will their converts. If those who lead people to Christ are Ishmaels, then they, too, become Ishmaels.

What I am describing is what happens when a spirit of enlistment replaces a spirit of repentance. That's why A.W. Tozer said, "The first call to the Church was not the great commission. Jesus first called the Church to prayer." He commanded them to go to Jerusalem and tarry there until they were endued with power from on high. He called them to go to the Upper Room before they were to spread the gospel. This is the basis of one of my favorite sayings: "We cannot deal with men about God until we have first dealt with God about man."

> My children, with whom I am again in labor until Christ is formed in you (Gal. 4:19).

By the time all the members of my family gave their lives to Christ, we had been told the message of salvation for four years. My oldest brother, who got saved first, had his whole Church praying for us. There were saints of God praying until Christ was formed in us. By the time we got saved, because of the prayers that went up for us, it was very clear to us what it meant to be a Christian. The seed found good soil. We took on the mind of Christ. We were spiritually born in God's timing.

We tend to think anything in the Church is Christian regardless of its birth. Whatever happened to the thought of praying until Christ is formed in the heart of that loved one. When I first started praying, I would go to bed by 10:00 p.m. I would rise at 3:00 a.m. and spend two hours each morning with God. At 5:00 a.m., I went back to bed. In those early morning hours I developed an intimate relationship with my God. I went from knowing about God to knowing God. One morning I had been praying for some time and I was getting tired. I had been praying for a particular family that I hadn't seen anything spiritual happen in anyway, so I said to the Lord, "I am really tired, I think I'll just go to bed. All I have been doing is praying for this family where nothing is happening anyway." As I told God that, the Holy Spirit spoke to my heart and said, "Ron you are the only person who will pray for that family, don't stop now." What if you are the only one who carries a burden for your family? Who will pray for them? Don't stop now!

We need to consider the words of a song by the late Keith Green: "My flesh is tired of seeking God but on my knees I'll stay." Only when we respond to God's call to prayer will we begin giving birth to Isaacs rather than Ishmaels.

SEVEN

THE ADULTEROUS GENERATION

We must remember that the gifts of the Holy Spirit are not the Holy Spirit Himself, nor are they Jesus or the Father.
—Cuthbert Wheaton

The Lord God has given me the tongue of the learned that I should know how to speak a word in season to him who is weary. He awakens me morning by morning, He awakens my ear (Isa. 50:4).

The tongue of the learned (or the tongue of the disciple, as some translations phrase it) is the tongue that speaks God's Word to the hearer. If I speak something in season, I say just what needs to be said exactly when it

89

needs to be said. To say anything in season is to say something when it is proper. If something comes out of season, it tends to be rejected even though it might be the right thing. In winter, when it snows in the upper Midwest, we may not necessarily like it, but we accept it and put up with it because we know that it is inevitable. It is part of the season. But if it was the middle of July, and we had a blizzard, that would be out of season. Even if we were in the middle of a drought, and we desperately needed moisture, we would reject snow in the middle of July because it would be out of season.

So speaking something in season deals with the spirit of a man. You can say the right thing the wrong way. Many preachers say things with such bombastic, arrogant spirits that people reject what they say even though what they say is correct. These preachers aren't sensitive to their hearers.

Sometimes, I take advantage of "red-eye specials," airplane flights that leave very early in the morning, and are consequently offered at a reduced price. You usually leave sometime between midnight and 2:00AM, but they are very peaceful flights. It's so dark out that you can't see the ground, so you don't know if you're crashing or not; that's nice. But the airlines generally go out of their way to make the flight conducive to sleeping. They turn down the lights and it's generally quiet. Rev. G. Raymond Carlson, the General Superintendent of the Assemblies of God, shared a story about a red-eye special that he took that wasn't so peaceful. It was very quiet except for a five-year-old girl traveling with her father. This little girl was continually fussing and whining. It was rather disruptive to the many passengers who were trying to sleep. Finally someone blurted out, "Can't you get her to shut up?" The man said he was sorry that his daughter was being a disturbance, but added that there were some mitigating circumstances. He said that while he and his family were on vacation, there was a terrible accident. The little girl's mother was in a casket in the cargo bay of the airplane.

As leaders, ministers and those who God would use to meet the needs of others, we need to be sensitive to their needs because we often do not realize what kind of cargo people are carrying. We don't know what's in the baggage department, so we need to be sensitive to the Spirit of God. But that sensitivity, that tongue of the learned or of the disciple, comes through discipline. We usually think of sensitivity as something mystical, so we try to tune into the spiritual realm in order to become more sensitive. Certainly the spiritual realm is involved, but we will only become sensitive to the voice of God through discipline; that is, through disciplining ourselves to pray.

"Disciple" finds its roots in the word "discipline." We must discipline ourselves in obedience to Christ if we are ever going to take on this ability to speak the right thing at the right time. The very nature of a spiritual leader is one who gives of himself. However, I have nothing of myself that is of any value to you at all. If I am going to lead spiritually, I must first be led spiritually. The true disciple is one who is led by his God.

Consider Jesus, our example. The verse above is taken from a chapter that prophesies about Jesus. That chapter goes on to explain how He would be handed over to evil men and how he would suffer many things at their hands. When we think of that verse in the context of Jesus' life, we see that Jesus was saying that His Father awakened Him morning by morning because Jesus was disciplined and responded to the call to prayer.

The true disciple cannot hesitate when the Lord calls him. Any hesitation to a call to prayer can actually quench the touch of God in one's life.

Behold, I Stand at the Door...

Dr. Wade Taylor has written a book entitled, *The Secret of the Stairs*. For a more thorough study of the Song of Solomon, I highly recommend this book.

> I was asleep, but my heart was awake. A voice! My beloved was knocking: 'Open to me, my sister, my darling, my dove, my perfect one! For my head is drenched with dew, my locks with the damp of the night.' I have taken off my dress. How can I put it back on again? I have washed my feet. How can I make them dirty again? (Song of Sol. 5:2,3).

This describes the interaction of the bride and the bridegroom. Spiritually, we Christians are the bride, and Jesus is the bridegroom. In these verses, the bride hears the voice of the groom calling to her, wanting to be with her. But the bride finds it inconvenient to respond to that call. Nothing could be more true today. Jesus is calling His bride to intimacy with Him. But when He calls us to intimacy (which we can experience only in prayer), we find it inconvenient. He often comes to us when we are the least willing to come to Him. He does this to see if we really care more for Him than we do for other things.

At the time the Song of Solomon was written, the floors were made of dirt, and the people wore open-toed sandals. As a result, their feet quickly became dirty, so this means that one would wash his feet before going to bed. The bride in these verses had already washed her feet, so she was reluctant to go to the door to let her lover in. First of all, she would have to get dressed. Then she would get her feet dirty all over again after having just washed them, meaning she would have to wash them again before going to bed. It would have been an inconvenience for her to respond.

When she said that she was asleep, but that her heart was awake, she meant that she was asleep physically, but awake and alive spiritually. Her heart was still quickened to Christ. She acknowledged her desire to be with Him, but she was not willing to respond immediately due to her present circumstances. The Church is in the same state today in regards to prayer. We want fellowship with God, but we will not be inconvenienced to gain it. Everyone will say, "Amen!" when a call to prayer is given, but no one will be inconvenienced to develop a prayer life.

My beloved extended his hand through the opening, and my feelings were aroused for him. I arose to open my beloved, and my hands dripped with myrrh, and my fingers with liquid myrrh, on the handles of the bolt. I opened to my beloved, but my beloved had turned away (Song of Sol. 5:4-6).

She hesitated to get up, but she sensed a certain presence. Then she saw his hand come through the door. In those days, there were no doorknobs. Instead, they had a hole, and to open the door, you reached through the opening and unfastened the latch. She saw him reach through, put his hand on the bolt, and that aroused her from her bed. She rushed to the door. When she put her hand on the latch of the door where her beloved's hand had been, there was a presence of God there. It is described by the myrrh of the groom's hand that was still there—even though he had left. She still felt His presence because she finally did respond to the call. However, she did not gain what she would have if she had not hesitated, for she discovered that He was gone.

This describes the two most common kinds of prayers we see today. The first kind responds to God in prayer only in the sense of the following verse.

Be anxious for nothing, but in everything, by prayer and supplication, let your requests be made known to God. And the peace of God, which surpasses all comprehension shall guard your hearts and minds in Christ Jesus (Phil. 4:6,7).

This kind of pray-er brings requests to God, asking God to take care of all of life's problems. He is not taken up with Christ or with His presence. His primary concern is his own supplications, thanksgiving and requests. And, in fulfillment of this Scripture, this pray-er does indeed sense the peace of God. Anytime we pray, we will receive a certain blessing and a certain perception of God's presence. He senses God's presence, just as the bride sensed His presence when she put her hand on the latch where His was. But there's a second kind of pray-er. This pray-er doesn't just experience God's presence, he experiences God, as the bride would have, if she had responded without hesitation, before the groom left. If the bride in the Song of Solomon had responded without hesitation, she would have experienced the Groom Himself, not just His presence.

Finally, brethren, whatever is true, whatever is honorable, whatever is right, whatever is pure, whatever is lovely, whatever is of good repute, if there is any excellence and if anything is worthy of praise, let your mind dwell on these things. The things you have learned and received and heard and seen in me, practice these things; and the God of peace shall be with you (Phil. 4:8,9).

These verses further clarify the difference between these two types of pray-ers. The one has a prayer life that is taken up with praying for things. That one is being Scriptural and isn't necessarily doing things the wrong way. But the other one has a prayer life that is taken up primarily with Christ Himself. This pray-er give himself over to what is pure. What is pure besides Jesus? He thinks on that which is true. What is true besides Jesus? He dwells on that which is virtuous. What is virtuous besides Jesus? It is really a description of God's character. It says that if you give yourself to that, the God of peace will be with you. The other one promises only the peace of God. Those who give themselves to the cares of this life in their prayer lives will experience the peace of God. But those who will give themselves to the pursuit of God Himself experience the God of peace. And there is a world of difference.

The problem is that we, having never experienced the God of peace, are satisfied with the peace of God. We don't know what we are missing. The difference between experiencing God and experiencing His peace is as great as the difference between what we can experience here on earth and what we will experience in heaven.

The Watchmen

The Song of Solomon indicates that those who are taken up with the peace of God rather than the God of peace are the watchmen of Jerusalem. They are the ones who are taken up with the work of the ministry. This doesn't mean that the ministry is wrong. We are to be giving ourselves in service to God, but the watchmen are the keepers of the vineyard. They are the ministers. But the Song of Solomon teaches us that there is a difference between the watchmen and the bride. The watchmen are the ones who are taken up with the cares of this life, but the bride is taken up with Jesus Himself. It's like the story of Mary and Martha. Mary wanted to be with Jesus, sitting in His presence and getting to know Him. Martha, on the other hand, was consumed with doing things for

Jesus and for others, but she had no time to just be with Him. Jesus wants our lives taken up with Him. That should be the primary focus of our prayer lives. After the pursuit of Christ takes priority in our prayer life we then make our requests and supplications.

In the Song of Solomon 5:6, the bride rushed out of the house when she realized that all she has was the myrrh on her hands. She wasn't satisfied with Christ's presence only. She ran out to search for Him, to seek Him. Then she ran into the watchmen, the ministers.

> The watchmen who make the rounds in the city found me. They struck me and wounded me. The guardsmen of the walls took away my shawl from me. "I adjure you, O daughters of Jerusalem, if you find my beloved, as to what you will tell him, for I am lovesick." "What kind of beloved is your beloved, O most beautiful among women? What kind of beloved is your beloved, thus you adjure us? (Song of Sol. 5:8,9).

The watchmen, representing God's ministers, are supposed to be the good guys in the sense that they are tending to the work of God. But they struck her. They wounded her. The wounds are insults that they hurl at her because they cannot understand her pursuit of Christ. She has a relationship with Him that most of the people couldn't understand, including the watchmen. They treated her as a fanatic, saying, "What is your beloved more than any other beloved?" They couldn't understand that a pursuit of God is more important than the work of God. So, they bruised her with their comments that Christ is not any more special than what they were doing.

It demonstrates how the work of God becomes more important to us than the God of the work. When the work of God takes that position of pre eminence, it literally becomes an idol and a false god, even though all this work is being done for God. If I refuse to follow Christ's call to prayer or intimacy but am still involved in the work of God, that work has become my idol because it has displaced Christ. I have seen many ministers become so taken up with God's work that they no longer have time to have a relationship with Him.

Seeking Signs or Seeking Jesus

We need to look at this in light of our current fascination with spiritual warfare.

Then some of the scribes and Pharisees answered Him, saying, "Teacher, we want to see a sign from You." But He answered and said to them, "An evil and adulterous generation craves for a sign, and yet none will be given to it but the sign of Jonah the prophet." (Matt. 12:38,39).

When the work of God has become an idol, it actually displaces our love for Christ, so that in the end, the work of God means more to us than our God does. When that is the case, signs and wonders become paramount. They become the things that we seek above all other things. In our thinking, it will make our work more effective. But Jesus says that the adulterous generation will receive only one sign: the sign of Jonah—repent. That is the sign of Jonah, and the adulterous generation needs to repent because it does not see Christ as the primary pursuit. But it must repent or face grave consequences.

The men of Nineveh shall stand up with this generation at the judgment, and shall condemn it because they repented at the preaching of Jonah;

and behold, something greater than Jonah is here (Matt. 12:41).

Jesus said that the men of Nineveh would condemn the adulterous generation because they repented at the preaching of Jonah, but the adulterous generation would not even repent at the preaching of God's own Son.

As Pentecostals, we have a rich heritage in signs and wonders. There's nothing wrong with them. In fact, the Church of Jesus Christ should manifest signs and wonders. However, when they become more to us than Christ Himself, we become adulterous. The same goes for any other ministry, doctrine or teaching. That's what Paul warned about in his letter to the Colossian believers.

Let no one keep defrauding you of your prize by delighting in false humility and the worship of angels, taking his stand on visions he has seen, inflated without cause by his fleshly mind (Col. 2:18).

Today doctrines of angels and demons have much more of our attention that Jesus Himself does. We are concentrating on angels and demons because we feel spiritual warfare is the call to the Church. In the process, we are becoming sidetracked where spiritual warfare is concerned. We can draw men out in droves to come and fight Satan, but we can't get handfuls to come out and pray to Jesus. Doesn't it seem like we have a problem when people are more enthused about Satan (even if it is only to fight him) than they are about Jesus?

I have talked to many people who are very interested and involved in so-called spiritual warfare. When you suggest that they need to just pursue God and develop a relationship with Him, they don't understand. They do not understand that a strong relationship with Christ will defeat Satan. Then, they strike you and give you a spiritual bruise, as the watchmen did to the bride in the Song of Solomon. They say that pursuing Jesus is not enough. They say you need to dispatch angels and do all sorts of other things. Jesus isn't enough.

> And then the seventy returned with joy, saying, "Lord, even the demons are subject to us in your name." And He said to them, "I was watching Satan fall from heaven like lightning. Behold, I have given you authority to tread upon serpents and scorpions and over all the power of the enemy, and nothing shall injure you. Nevertheless, do not rejoice in this, that the spirits are subject to you, but rejoice that your names are recorded in heaven" (Luke 10:17-20).

The disciples of Jesus were also very excited about demons and about the power they had over them. They were a lot like many disciples in our churches today. But Jesus knew their hearts, and He knew that their focus was off-center, so He said in essence, "Big deal. That's nothing. I saw Satan himself fall from heaven. And the half has not been told about the power I have given you. You will be able to tread upon serpents and scorpions, and nothing shall harm you. That should be business as usual for those who believe in Me. But don't rejoice in this, but rejoice that your names are recorded in heaven."

If I come to the place in my spiritual life where all I can rejoice in is my power over the enemy, then I have lost my perspective. I'm not making Christ my pursuit. I'm making the work of God my pursuit, and I need signs and wonders to make that effective.

Now when the unclean spirit goes out of a man, it passes through waterless places, seeking rest and does not find it. Then it says, 'I will return to my house from which I came'; and when it finds it unoccupied, swept, and put in order, then it goes and takes along with it seven other spirits more wicked than itself, and they go and live there; and the last state of that man will be worse than the first. That is the way it will also be with this evil generation" (Matt. 12:43-45).

There is power in the name of Jesus. Even the adulterous generation has the power to deliver someone in the name of Jesus. (Remember that Jesus said that many would come to Him after this life and would say, "Lord, Lord, did we not prophecy in Your name, and in Your name cast out demons, and in Your name perform many miracles?" but He will say to them, "Depart from me. I never knew you." [See Matthew 7:21-24]). This generation seeks spiritual power. Then they take this power to do the work of God. They may cast out a demon. But they are still adulterous. Signs, wonders and power mean as much or more to them than Christ.

This doesn't mean they don't love Jesus. I would suppose that they do, but an adulterer is what he is because he has more than one lover. This generation loves Jesus, but He isn't their only lover or their greatest lover. Jesus is not the primary pursuit of their lives. As a result, they do not have the ability to create a hunger and a thirsting for Jesus in their converts. They may cast a demon out of a man, and they may make him a convert, but he will not hunger and thirst for Jesus anymore than they do. The demon that left the man may well return again to find his house cleaned and swept, but if that man is not taken up with a pursuit of Christ, then it will come back seven times worse. The final state of that man is worse than if we hadn't done anything to set him free.

It's one thing to clean house, but if you don't continue to saturate it with prayer and develop within it a hunger for Jesus, it can end up seven times worse than when you first began. The adulterous generation can cause more trouble than good because it doesn't produce a passionate desire for Jesus.

Nurturing the Saints

This brings us back to the Song of Solomon. The bride realized that she must pursue the groom more than anything else. Because of making intimacy with Christ her first priority she gained that which is necessary to help nurture others toward a deeper relationship with Christ. The Song of Solomon often refers to the woman's breast. However, it is always referred to as a nurturing agent.

> We have a young sister, and her breasts are not yet grown. What shall we do for our sister for the day she is spoken for? If she is a wall, we will build towers of silver on her. If she is a door, we will enclose her with panels of cedar. I am a wall, and my breasts are like towers. Thus I have become in his eyes like one bringing contentment (Song of Sol. 8:8-10).

The reference to the young sister's breasts being small means that she does not have the ability to nurture others in the things of the Lord. The bride then begins to make suggestions as to what can be done to help her. "If she is a wall, we will build towers of silver on her."

The wall represents someone who is solid in their

doctrine. Having done all, they stand. They are no longer tossed to and fro by every wind of doctrine. However, they may be solid in their Bible knowledge but they have no prayer life. Therefore, they lack the ability to cause others to long for what they have. The suggestion is then made that they build towers of silver on her. They want her to shine so that others will see her and long to have what she has. The wall has the word of God down but has no intimacy, therefore, it lacks the glow of the Holy Spirit. The mature bride was a wall and her breasts were like towers. Not only was she solid in her knowledge of God's Word, but she also had a deep prayer life. That produced in her what others would long for.

The bride goes on to say that if the young sister was a door that they would enclose her with panels of cedar. The door represented something that was unstable. In her day all doors were double hinged and could swing either way. This dealt with her instability in the Word of God. She needed someone to teach her the elementary truths of God's Word. That teaching would enclose her with panels of cedar.

It is very important to realize that the bride's pursuit of Jesus only, developed in her a concern for others who are not mature in the things of God. Once her relationship with Christ developed, her desire for others to experience the same thing grew. Therefore, a pursuit of Christ will accomplish the Work of God. However, it will accomplish it in such a manner that your disciples will gain a hunger and thirst for Jesus. There will be no fear of the clean house being repossessed by the same evil spirit that was previously cast out.

The adulterous generation, a generation taken up with signs and wonders more so than Jesus, cannot create a hunger for Jesus in her disciples. It is important to note that the adulterous generation is not necessarily a prayerless generation. It's just that their prayer life is that of getting things from Jesus rather than Jesus himself.

Jesus wants us flowing in the Spirit, Jesus wants us to operate in the gifts, but He doesn't want those things to displace our love for Him. The gifts of the Spirit and spiritual warfare should just be another part of my life which has its focus on Jesus first.

EIGHT

CONTROLLING SPIRITS

I will learn the secret of creation, and be myself
like God.
—Dr. Victor Frankenstein

In Mary Shelly's classic novel, *Frankenstein*, the brilliant young Dr. Frankenstein was victimized by his own
lust for power. He wanted the power to control life and
death by creating a life, a life that would be immortal,
never subject to death or the ravages of old age. His older,
wiser professors warned him not to pursue such matters
because "...There are some things man was not meant to
know." But the brash young man dismissed their words
as so much rubbish and went on to pursue his dream: to
control the power of creation. As we all know, his inflated
opinion of himself and his obsessions led him down a

road of pain, sorrow, bloodshed and death. In his arrogant zeal to control God's wondrous power of creation, he succeeded only in creating a monster.

Although Shelly's book is just a horror yarn, it does accurately depict one recurring theme in man's history: man's desire to be like God, to have at least just a taste of God's omnipotent power to control. Invariably his striving to reach this dizzying height has resulted in disaster. Each man's attempts to do so have resulted in him creating his own monster. Satan, being aware of man's carnal desire to control, has always been at man's side, encouraging him to pursue that desire by appealing to his flesh. The first and most famous incident occurred in the Garden of Eden.

> And the serpent said to the woman, "You surely shall not die! For God knows that in the day you eat from it, your eyes will be opened and you will be like God, knowing good and evil (Gen. 3:4,5).

The serpent was appealing to a desire already brewing in the heart of man. The man and woman God placed in the Garden had a desire to be like God before the serpent entered into the picture. If they hadn't already had such a desire, the serpent's suggestions wouldn't have been tempting; they couldn't be tempted by something they didn't want. Satan just played on man's wish to be like God, to be able to control his own destiny, a thought that has captured the minds of men literally since the beginning of time.

However, man's insatiable appetite for control goes beyond just controlling his own destiny. Throughout the annals of recorded time, he has endeavored to control the destinies of his fellow man as well, another attempt at being like God, who controls the destiny of all creation. Satan concentrated on this desire when he tempted Jesus.

Again the devil took him to a very high mountain, and showed Him all the kingdoms of the world, and their glory; and he said to Him, "All these things I will give you, if you fall down and worship me" (Matt. 4:8,9).

Satan's entire game is control. Satan didn't only offer Jesus the opportunity to control all the kingdoms of the world—he also tried to gain control of Jesus by getting Jesus to worship him. Satan was hoping he could appeal to Jesus' human nature and its inclination to control. He failed miserably with Jesus. He failed because of Jesus' most confusing quality: He was a humble servant. This confused everybody, even Jesus' disciples. They couldn't understand why Jesus, the King, would serve instead of being served. Most men want to be served, and being served tends to promote pride. Very few men will be servants, which is unfortunate since serving makes one humble. Man's general aversion to serving makes the gentle humility of Jesus shine like a candle in the darkness of humanity.

But Satan has enticed many others throughout the centuries with his illusion of control. Now is no exception. One of the primary goals of occultists is to control; to control their lives and the lives of those around them. Without a doubt, the desire to control is Satanic in nature.

Perceiving the Spiritual Realm, or Controlling it?

The human brain has the capacity to perceive two images simultaneously: one image from the physical world and one image from the spiritual realm. Some believers refer to this second image as a vision. Some occultists refer to it as an out of the body experience. The difference between the two is the source transmitting the spiritual image: is it God, or is it Satan? I remember once

God caused me to see the spiritual bondage a certain community was suffering from at the same time I was driving my car down a street in that area. I was aware of the physical world around me and able to operate my car without any impairment of my senses. At the same time, I was aware of the spiritual realm surrounding me.

The goal of the occultist is to have a spiritual revolving door. That is, to perceive the spiritual realm at will, whenever one wishes to do so. When you get right down to the heart of the matter, it is a desire to control one's interaction with the spiritual realm. I don't find this particularly alarming; it is no more than I would expect from occultists. However, I am alarmed by Christians who are seeking their own "Christian" revolving door. They want to control their interaction with the spiritual realm every bit as much as the occultists do.

Many Christians, enticed by our sinful nature's desire to control, are trying to control the gifts of the Holy Spirit. They want to function in those gifts at a moment's notice, at their convenience. They want to determine when God will speak to them, when they will see a vision or when they will prophecy. This is a very serious error. It makes man the master, making the decisions, controlling the situation, when he should be the servant. Those who truly serve God give Him control. And in the end, through this surrender, they ultimately gain control.

And the spirits of prophets are subject to prophets (1 Cor. 14:32).

If I am being used in some gift of the Holy Spirit, I have control of that gift. It does not control me. I can refuse to speak in tongues. I can refuse to utter a word of prophecy. In that sense, we control the gift. But what I am talking about is controlling the administration of that gift. This means making it available at my discretion and using it as my personal gift. So those who really give themselves to God find that they actually gain control. On the other hand, those who serve Satan seek to gain control, and, through that, they have lost control. The more you give yourself to God, the more God gives you Himself, which is life. The more you give yourself to Satan, the more he gives you of himself, which is death. That is the basic difference between those who serve God and those who serve Satan.

As children of God, we are first and foremost servants. God is the master. He will decide when and if to use me in certain gifts of the Holy Spirit. It is not my choice or yours. We are to be ready in season and out, having our senses trained, prepared to be used by God whenever He chooses. If at any time we find ourselves controlling the gifts of the Spirit, we'd better wake up. If we can control them, then the Holy Spirit is not involved—we are using an unholy spirit.

Using An Unholy Spirit to Control

It must be understood that the desire to control is not just another part of the Christian life. Only our sinful nature wants to control others. When we gave our lives over to Jesus, we gave up control of our lives, and we gave up the control we exercised over others. When we met Christ, we realized that we didn't know what was best for us and for others—He alone did (and He still does). That's why we gave Him control over all of our decisions and even control over our loved ones. Because He knows best, He alone is to have control.

But, after years of being saved, after losing touch with God through a lack of prayer, that sinful human nature emerges again with its desire to control. Slowly we begin to control again. Our lives. The lives of others. Situations. As things snowball, we end up controlling everything—

or at least trying.

I've heard some people express the opinion that one person can't really control another person, at least not without using superior physical force against someone. The truth of the matter is people control other individuals and whole groups every day in our society, without using a pistol or a broadsword. I've seen it happen many times. In fact, I've had other people control me—sometimes before I knew what was happening.

It is very simple to control others through our attitudes. Many times I have been in situations where a person in the group I'm speaking to has a spirit contrary to mine. When I'm teaching, my thoughts keep centering on that person. I keep thinking, "How's he going to respond to this?" and "What kind of argument is he going to use to dispute this point?" In such a situation, that one contentious individual is controlling me through his contrary spirit. When you're in that sort of position, they end up capturing most of your attention and you end up doing things that person's way. It's all caused by a controlling spirit, an unholy spirit.

I recall one specific occasion when I was trying to teach a Sunday School class which included someone with a controlling spirit. The class had not begun yet. An elderly couple, unremarkable to look at, came in and inconspicuously found seats. But, when I began teaching, the woman refused to look at me. As she sat there glaring at the Sunday School handout, I thought she might actually ignite it with the intensity of her gaze. It was plain to me that she didn't like what I was saying. I wasn't the only one who noticed her, either. It was obvious, as well as disruptive, to the whole class. She was trying to control what went on in class through her attitude.

I know of other people who have faced the same kind of control problems. I know one pastor who had to deal with a couple in his church who did not see eye-to-eye with him at all. They didn't believe the same way he did, nor did they subscribe to his doctrine. After talking to him about this once, he reached into one of his desk drawers and pulled out a whole series of teachings he intended to use to counter everything this couple was saying. That one couple had such a contrary spirit that they were actually controlling their pastor with it. He was directing all his teachings at that one couple, even though he had a congregation of several hundred people.

There are many such methods people use to control others. Everybody knows at least one person who always gets his way because of his temper. Such a person quickly realizes that it is not even necessary to really be angry in order to get his way. He sees that a sufficient display of anger will do the trick. It's also very common for some to use sickness as a means of controlling others. Some control by simple, blunt intimidation. Others use a more complex, refined sense of superiority to cause others to react in a way desired. All these various ways of controlling people are not the result of the Holy Spirit in one's life, but are, rather, the result of an unholy spirit.

Goal: Profits or Prophets?

False prophets often operate out of a spirit of jealousy or envy. Even believers in Christ can open themselves up to Satanic influence through a jealous spirit. It has happened before. In Acts 8:9-24, we read the account of Simon the magician. Simon regularly performed astonishing feats of magic. So breathtaking were they that he became known as "the Great Power of God." Simon relished his ability to influence and control those around him. In the height of his fame, however, something peculiar happened. Upon hearing the preaching of Peter, he believed and was baptized. Simon travelled with the apostles after that, and he envied their ability to perform great miracles.

One day, he approached Peter and asked if Peter would sell him the power to perform miracles and cause people to receive the baptism of the Holy Spirit. Peter's response seems very severe, especially considering that Simon was a believer. Peter said, "May your silver perish with you because you thought you could obtain the gifts of God with money." Noticing Simon's envious spirit, Peter discerned that his heart was not right with God. Being willing to pay money for a gift indicates a covetous spirit or a jealous heart. It indicates that someone is more interested in receiving gifts from God than he is in having a relationship with God. Anyone who would be so willing to offer money for God's gifts has a heart that wants to control others, not a heart that simply wants God.

> Pursue love, yet desire earnestly spiritual gifts, but especially that you may prophesy (1 Cor. 14:1).

Paul instructed his readers to desire spiritual gifts. It's not wrong to desire them. It's exactly right to desire them. However, Paul also said that without love, one is nothing. Without love, those gifts are worthless. Without love, a desire for spiritual gifts is nothing more than spiritual greed and a desire to control others through the exercise of spiritual gifts.

I have heard of schools that train people to be prophets. I believe most of these "schools for prophets" should be renamed "schools for profits." We can't hope to make a prophet through making a profit. If Simon the sorcerer lived today, he probably wouldn't have been rebuked. If he had his Visa or Mastercard with him, they would have shipped him off so he could buy the "gift" of prophecy. And it is beyond me how anyone can justify exacting a fee for a spiritual gift. To begin with, a spiritual gift is given by God. There is no other source. Men simply can't bestow spiritual gifts. And they certainly can't go around peddling them. There is no Biblical basis for paying for spiritual gifts. Actually the contrary is what you find in Scripture. The very fact that they're called "gifts" argues against paying for them.

Paying a fee for Biblical training is an entirely different category altogether. A calling is different than a gift. Even if God calls me to be a prophet, I cannot pay a price to become one. A calling has to be developed and nurtured through prayer, the Word, and experience. God may call someone to be a pastor. He may go to Bible college and graduate. However, he does not become one by paying for his training. He becomes one as the ministry shapes him.

The Bible teaches us that if one if jealous of another man's ministry, his jealous spirit can open him up to Satanic influences, rather than God's. He can then be used by Satan to prophecy through an unholy spirit. So the best you could ever have is a "school for false prophets."

Truth Not Admissible as a Defense

And it happened that as we were going to the place of prayer, a certain slave-girl having a spirit of divination met us, who was bringing her masters much profit by fortunetelling. Following after Paul and us, she kept crying out, saying, "These men are bond-servants of the Most High God, who are proclaiming to you the way of salvation" (Acts 16:16,17).

This is very interesting. The Bible tells us that this woman was a fortuneteller, but it also tells us that she was proclaiming the truth about the message of salvation. She was speaking the truth about the gospel! How could that be occultic? Was she, then, a Christian fortuneteller?

And she continued doing this for many days. But Paul was greatly annoyed, and turned and said to the spirit, "I command you in the name of Jesus Christ to come out of her!" And it came out at that very moment (Acts 16:18).

That woman was being used by an unholy spirit. Although on the surface it may have appeared to be of God, it was really of Satan. She did prophesy correctly about the things of God, but it was the work of an evil spirit just the same. This proves we can be used by an unholy spirit and can prophesy correctly. But before we can delve into this further, we need to take a look at the power of jealousy and envy.

Jealous Is as Jealous Does

Paul wrote to the believers in Corinth that he had problems with men who were intensely jealous. They wanted to be apostles like him, probably because they coveted the respect that was accorded Paul in the Church. Paul refused to allow them the occasion because of their jealous motives. They wanted to move in on Paul's ministry. Their envious spirits were opening a door for Satan, disguising himself as an angel of light, to use them. Paul was undaunted, though.

But what I am doing I will continue to do, that I may cut off opportunity to be regarded just as we are in the matter about which they are boasting. For such men are false apostles, deceitful workers, disguising themselves as apostles of Christ. And no wonder, for even Satan disguises himself as an angel of light. Therefore, it is not surprising if his servants also disguise themselves as servants of righteousness whose end shall be according to their deeds (2 Cor. 11:12-15).

Through a jealous or envious spirit, a man opens his own spirit to be influenced by Satan. Then Satan can operate through him by means of an unholy spirit's occultic powers. There is an obvious ministry of God's Holy Spirit that is right and proper for today. However, there can just as easily be an unholy spirit which can imitate the Holy Spirit.

The jealous or envious spirit concentrates entirely on self and, consequently, self-aggrandizement. Much of the emphasis in ministry today is on gain, just as it was for the masters of the slave-girl in Acts 16. After Paul had cast the demon out of that girl, her masters were angry. Without the demon, she couldn't prophesy any more. That meant a loss of revenue for them, so they dragged Paul and Silas off to the authorities. I see a lot of personal prophecy today that, through the control of individuals, is causing a lot of personal profits.

Familiar Spirits

Satan can and often does masquerade as an angel of light. When he does this, he looks harmless enough. In fact, he appears very benevolent. He poses as one who has good wishes for all. Many don't see through his disguise or realize what is under it: a roaring lion, seeking whom he may devour; one who has been a liar from the beginning and who seeks only to kill, to steal and to destroy. In his many centuries of tormenting man, he has found it most effective.

So it shouldn't come as any surprise that his confederates use the same techniques. Demonic spirits often try to impersonate the Holy Spirit. They easily fool believers who are filled with jealousy, envy or pride. These familiar spirits, as they are called, can deceive a false prophet into thinking that what they are telling him is from God.

Familiar spirits, unlike hindering spirits, are not overtly destructive. A familiar spirit does very little besides observe a person. It learns all there is to learn about that individual, then reports back to Satan. Since Satan is neither omnipresent nor omniscient, he depends on the familiar spirits assigned to each person to inform him when he acts as the accuser of the brethren.

These familiar spirits also act to validate the occult. For instance, a familiar spirit which has observed a person from birth to death can respond to the summons of a seance, in which people attempt to contact the spirit of a deceased friend or loved one. The demon, after spending decades watching the deceased person in question, can easily imitate that person's voice and provide details of his life that will convince the people that the spirit is their dearly departed lost acquaintance.

Similarly, these familiar spirits can inspire a false prophet to prophecy over someone while providing uncanny details about that person's life that the false prophet would have no way of knowing. On the surface, it appears to be a manifestation of God's power when really it is a familiar spirit masquerading as an angel of light. You have to be careful. As Ralph M. Riggs has stated, "It is a false reverence which accepts everything which purports to be a divine message as if it were from God directly and without human admixture."[1]

So how can you tell if a message is from God? To begin with, you must go beyond the appearances at the surface. You must get down to the motivation of the prophet. In the Bible, God's prophets never desired glory, acclaim or reverence from man. They didn't seek to build a reputation for being "spiritual." In fact, in their humility, they usually didn't want to be the ones who gave the message of God to the people. Their only desire was to glorify God, and that was why they spoke God's messages. They didn't do it to build their reputation with man. The false prophet, however, thrives on the attention and praises of man. He wants everyone to regard him as an awesome spiritual leader, unlike the prophet who only wants everyone to love the Lord their God with all their being. In his pursuit of popularity, the false prophet takes on the very nature of Satan.

Satanic Nature

How you have fallen from heaven, O star of the morning, son of the dawn! You have been cut down to the earth, you who have weakened the nations! But you have said in your heart, "I will ascend to heaven; I will raise my throne above the stars of God, and I will sit on the mount of assembly in the recesses of the north. I will ascend the heights of the clouds; I will make myself like the Most High." Nevertheless, you will be thrust down to Sheol, to the recesses of the pit (Isa. 14:12-15).

Although I believe this verse if referring to Satan, I am aware that not everyone concurs. Some believe that Isaiah was speaking about one of the monarchs of his era. It really doesn't make any difference who Isaiah was referring to. The point is the same in either case; any person who desires to exalt himself is satanic in nature. The entire message of the cross of Christ is death to self, not self-exaltation.

False prophets always act out of a desire to exalt themselves. Take Diotrephes, for example. In the New Testament, the apostle John wrote a message to one of the churches, and that message contradicted what the false prophet Diotrephes was teaching.

I wrote something to the church; but Diotrephes, who loves to be first among them, does not accept what we say. For this reason, if I come, I will call attention to his deeds which he does, unjustly accusing us with wicked words; and not satisfied with this, neither does he himself receive the brethren, and he forbids those who desire to do so, and puts them out of the church. Beloved, do not imitate what is evil, but what is good. The one who does good is of God; the one who does evil has not seen God (3 John 9-11).

How did Diotrephes respond to John's correction? As is the case with any person, when Diotrephes was corrected, his true nature came out. He lashed out at him and began slandering the apostle. He was angry because he knew John's message, which didn't agree with his, would cause others to see that Diotrephes was a false prophet and that he wasn't hearing from God. People would no longer revere and respect him as a great spiritual man. His response was one of pride, and pride is the very essence of Satan's nature. That evil nature will not accept correction. But Christ's nature is humility, which quietly accepts and appreciates correction.

This portion of Scripture gives us a glimpse into Satan's hideous nature. It describes three specific ways that his nature is revealed, and, by inference, provides three specific ways for us to identify it. Being able to identify Satan's nature means being able to identify false prophets and thereby identify and avoid false doctrines.

Self-Exaltation

Lucifer's self-exaltation, a by-product of his great pride, was one of the key reasons that he was banished from heaven and from God's service. He lifted himself up and in his mind displaced the Creator of all things who made him and loved him. There's an old saying which tells us, "The apple doesn't fall very far from the tree," and it is very applicable to Satan and his servants, who act with his nature. Like the devil, they, too, will seek to exalt themselves.

Often this is not easy to identify, though. If someone gave a word of prophecy which only extolled the virtues and greatness of the "prophet," it would be easy to see that person was exalting himself. But I don't think it's likely you'll hear something like that. It would be too easy to identify as false, and that's exactly what Satan doesn't want, so he'll make it as subtle as possible.

A man with a satanic nature can seem to be operating in the gifts of the Holy Spirit, appearing as if he has only God's best interests at heart, when really he does not. Personal prophecy can look very innocent, and when it is properly used it is innocent. However, the "prophet" can very easily have ulterior motives. He may be very careful not to mention himself or do anything that appears to exalt himself, but the very fact that he perceives himself as the messenger of God provides an exaltation of its own. He thinks others perceive him as one who is close to God, elevating him, a "prophet," above other men.

Sowing Dissension

Clearly this is a matter of a person's heart. A "prophet's" desire for self-exaltation may be carefully concealed. The way you can tell if a person is out for self-exaltation is that when he is corrected, he will respond as Diotrephes did. He won't be able to receive that correction because it is humbling. Immediately Diotrephes began to spread rumors about John and his associates. John wrote in verse ten that he knew Diotrephes was "unjustly accusing us with wicked words..."

We're not the only ones who know that a house divided against itself cannot stand. Satan knows it, too. That is why he seeks to gain control over those in the Church (if they will yield control to him). Then, once he has infiltrated the Church, he sets about trying to cause a split. If he cannot render a church powerless through false teaching, then he will inspire someone to spread falsehoods with "wicked words" in hopes of causing those who believe in the truth to leave the church.

I saw Satan operate this way early in my ministry. A young girl came to our church asking us to help deliver her from demonic possession. She had been a practicing witch. The pastor and the board spent hours casting demon after demon from her. After this had gone on for several weeks, it was revealed that she was actually planted in our church by her coven in order to cause dissension. She had no interest in deliverance. She was just trying to infiltrate our church. As soon as her true motives were exposed, she set about spreading malicious lies about the senior pastor's wife. She said, for instance, that the pastor's wife was a lesbian. That, of course, was a lie that was targeted at dividing the church.

I've heard of similar circumstances at other churches. In one incident, a woman was praying over a person who had come to the alter to seek God's help in an urgent matter. The woman began to prophecy over this individual, but her prophecy was completely irrelevant. It had nothing to do with this person. The pastor's wife knew what this person's problem was and knew that this woman's prophecy was completely off base, so she approached her later on. The correction infuriated this woman. She was so overcome with rage that she began to spread false rumors about the pastor's son, claiming he was a homosexual. It is typical for those influenced by an unholy spirit to cause division once they are found out.

Imitating Evil

Evil is the most obvious trait of Satan, and you can be sure that his servants will imitate evil. Even as John admonished his readers, "Beloved, do not imitate what is evil..." so also Satan encourages those who serve his purposes to practice evil.

We seem unable to believe that even believers can be used by Satan. The Scriptures warn believers over and over to be careful so as not to imitate evil and thus be used by Satan.

> If a prophet or a dreamer of dreams arises among you and gives you a sign or wonder, and the sign or wonder comes true, concerning which he spoke to you saying, "Let us go after other gods (whom you have known) and let us serve them," you shall not listen to the words of that prophet or that dreamer of dreams; for the Lord your God is testing you to find out if you love the Lord your God with all your heart and with all your soul (Deut. 13:1-3).

Sometimes evil doesn't look like evil right away. Prophecy may come true or a vision may come to pass, but that doesn't legitimize it. The false prophet can tap into the spirit realm and actually perform miracles. However, he is using the miracle to subtly turn us from the one true God. He's not going to come out and say, "Come on, let's go serve other gods!" He first uses his miraculous powers to convince us that he speaks for God.

> When you enter the land which the Lord your God is giving you, you shall not learn to imitate the detestable things of those nations. There shall not be found among you anyone who makes his

son or his daughter pass through fire, one who uses divination, one who practices witchcraft, or one who interprets omens, or a sorcerer, or one who casts a spell, or a medium (familiar spirit) or a spiritist, or one who calls up the dead. For whoever does these things is detestable to the Lord... (Deut. 18:9-12).

God knew that is is possible for His people to imitate the evil practices of the false prophet. That is why he prohibited his people from doing so (He wouldn't forbid them to do something they can't do in the first place, would He?). Any believer who allows himself to become entrenched in envy opens himself up to satanic forces and is in danger of becoming a false prophet.

I will raise up a prophet from among their countrymen like you, and I will put My words in his mouth, and he shall speak to them all that I command him. (Deut. 18:18).

There is such a thing as a true prophet just as there is such a thing as a true personal prophecy. Only the true prophet speaks only what God has put in his mouth.

And you may say in your heart, 'How shall we know the word which the Lord has not spoken?' (Deut. 18:21).

That is the great question of our day. How do we know what is of the Lord and what is not? How do we know good from evil? The answer is found in the next verse.

When a prophet speaks in the name of the Lord, if the thing does not come about or come true, that is the thing which the Lord has not spoken (Deut. 18:22).

The test for the true prophet was whether or not one-hundred percent of his prophecies came true. If they did not come to pass, they were not of God and the prophet was considered a medium or a spiritist (Leviticus 20:27). The consequences for being proved guilty of this were very serious too. If their prophesies did not come true, they were stoned to death. The true prophet never erred because he spoke God's words. When a prophet erred, he was put to death because they recognized that he operated out of occultic powers and not God's.

The Word and Doctrine

The purest doctrines come out of the repentant heart because it is humble. However, the false prophet has no interest in repentance or in humility, so his doctrine is not pure. Instead it is cluttered with the same haughtiness that clutters his heart. And it is this haughty doctrine which discredits him. It has never been enough for a prophet to just acknowledge God. His doctrine must conform to what is right and pure. In the Old Testament this was true. "A prophet might allege that he spoke in the name of Yahweh, but if he did not acknowledge the authority of Moses and subscribe to the doctrines of the Exodus, he was a false prophet."[2]

It is the rejection of our own doctrines that has caused the Pentecostal Church to be filled with false prophets. The pure doctrines that were established by repentant hearts during our revival at the turn of the century, have been abandoned. We have left the doctrine of the cross of Christ which promotes the denial of self. In its place, we have doctrines which stress our rights to comfort and luxury. The Church in the United States spends more time and money pampering herself than anything else.

If we do not hold on to our pure doctrines, the Spirit of God will not function among us. Consider the Laodicean Church which Jesus addressed in the Book of Revelations. He shows us a wealthy, confident church which boasts, "I am rich and have need of nothing." It was a church which had a full treasury inside, but which had left Jesus outside. They had left the doctrine of self-denial, so anything that took place in that church in the name of prophecy was not inspired by God's Spirit, but by a false spirit. The true Spirit of God would not operate in any church which Jesus said he would spew out of his mouth.

Although one-hundred percent accuracy was an important test of a prophet during the Old Testament period, by far the most important test centered around the theology. Moses established the theological norm in Deuteronomy 13. In the New Testament, Jesus became the norm for all Christian prophets. Therefore, any prophetic message that maligns the position or power of Christ must be refuted because it is founded on a doctrine that is contrary to the nature of Christ.

We tend to make the issue of discernment so mystical and spiritual that no one can understand it. Discernment would be difficult if we had no standard by which to judge things. However, we have a wonderful standard; Jesus. Discernment is that of comparing everything we see or hear to Jesus. Without prayer this is a very difficult thing to do. Prayer puts us in the presence of Jesus on a daily basis. It makes us familiar with His nature and character. Through prayer, discernment is actually quite simple. When you hear a man prophesy you pick up on his spirit and compare it to Jesus' spirit. You listen to his message and see if it is contrary to the nature of Christ.

While Jesus was on earth, he had to deal with a horrendously corrupt religious system. The conservative Pharisees were no better than the liberal Saducees. Together the two groups, both espousing (but not truly practicing) the Law of Moses, formed a religious system which wreaked of hypocrisy and corruption. Most of Jesus' preaching was intended to correct these people who had left the basic principles of their own beliefs. His message was one of repentance, the single doctrine which is crucial to any prophet.

Jeremiah felt that the doctrine of repentance was the only test of a prophet. As far as he was concerned, a prophet was false when he failed to preach repentance to a corrupt people. "The prophet Jeremiah proposes no test for a prophet based on the techniques he follows nor the external trappings of his ministry. Rather the crux of Jeremiah's message is this: the false prophet is one who lives an immoral, unethical life. For Jeremiah, the false prophet was one who lived immorally and proclaimed a message of false optimism in a time when optimism was unwarranted. Jeremiah depicts the behavior of the false prophet this way: `They keep saying to those who despise Me (i.e., the Lord), "The Lord says: You will have peace." And to all who follow the stubbornness of their hearts they say, "No harm will come to you." ' "³

I heard a story about a Christian woman who divorced her husband because he could not afford to support the kind of lifestyle she wanted. After she had done away with him, she went off to find a personal prophet to prophesy over her. The personal prophet "prophesied" over her telling her God wanted her happy and that she should go off and find a man who could take care of her the way she wanted to be taken care of. Even though she was following the stubbornness of her own heart, that "prophet" said, "The Lord will give you peace." Jeremiah considered that false prophecy. Consolation and promises of peace were given where repentance was needed. The true prophet preaches the simple message of repentance.

The truth of this statement impacted me when I was teaching a seminar at a small church in Colorado. The teaching became intense as I dealt with the sin of prayerlessness. God was dealing with the stubborn hearts of those who refused to spend time with Jesus. After I described the predicament which prayerlessness has placed us in, I asked, "What is the solution to this problem?" The room became very silent. Then a woman from the back of the church spoke up. "Repentance," she said. Then she broke into tears and wept before the Lord. She was being a prophet of God at that time, for God put that single word in her mouth, and it penetrated the spirits of all of us in the room.

What is the message of the Spirit today? What do you imagine God's Spirit is saying to a church where minister after minister is running off with church secretary after church secretary; where our church kids dance, drink, rock and roll, and do drugs, all in the name of Jesus, and where church officials show more concern over salaries than over souls? The message is "Repent." But we do not need to repent of these outward actions. We need to repent of what is causing these actions: prayerlessness.

It is the only way to free ourselves of the spirit of control which has gripped us. It has led us to try to control our destinies, other people and even our God. It's time to return to the Master. It's time to relinquish control to Him once again.

Hebrews 5:12-14 tells us to have our sensitivity to the spirit sharpened. We can learn to discern good from evil by reason of use. The "reason of use" is prayer. Spending time in Christ's presence sharpens our ability to tell if someone is of God or not. Unless the Church returns to prayer, she will never sharpen her ability to discern good from evil. And lacking that, she will eventually unknowingly be sucked down into the evil she cannot perceive.

FOOTNOTES

[1]Ralph M. Riggs. *The Spirit Himself* (Springfield, MO.: Gospel Publishing House, 1949), pp. 159, 160.

[2]J.S. Motyer, *"Prophecy, Prophet," The New Bible Dictionary,* ed. J.D. Douglas (Grand Rapids: William B. Eerdmans Publishing Co., 1962) pp. 1042.

[3]Timothy M. Powell, Ph.D., *Paraclete* (Springfield, MO: Gospel Publishing House, 1983) pp. 15.

NINE

WORSHIPOLATRY

Tis mad idolatry to make the service greater than
the god.
—William Shakespeare, *Troilus and Cressida*

It was a beautiful seventy-five degrees. The beauty of
the cloudless azure sky seemed to be actually singing
praises to the Creator who made it. On my left, the Rocky
Mountains stretched across the horizon, a monument to
the greatness of the Lord of heaven and earth. The scenery
seemed to join in harmony with the anointed worship
music I was listening to. As I drove, I could sense the
presence of God surrounding me. I was driving through
Colorado en route to my next prayer seminar at a church
in North Dakota, and everything seemed to be going my
way. I had just finalized the details for another book with
my publisher. My wife and I were planning our vacation.
Life was a joy—and then I saw it.

I had never seen a house in such a state. It looked like the devil himself lived there. The sparse vegetation in the yard resembled nothing I had every seen. Old cars were scattered around the yard. It looked like they had just dropped out of the sky, landing randomly and showering the area with tailpipes, radiators and an assortment of automotive shrapnel. In fact, that seemed to be a likely hypothesis. It didn't look like they had been driven there; not one of them had a single wheel. The landscape was dotted with the owner's private collection of beer cans. The outside of the house was adorned with several colors of spray paint and an equal number of unusual (if profane) slogans. It seemed like the spray paint may have been all that was holding the old hovel together. The financial and spiritual need of the occupants was obviously great.

As I drove by, the Holy Spirit spoke to my heart, saying something that would later have a significant impact on my life and ministry. He said, **"The world is dying without Jesus, and all the Church is doing is singing songs."** I reached over and turned down the volume of my car stereo. The worship and praise music was suddenly too loud. I must have misunderstood what the Holy Spirit was saying to me. Then He said once more, a little more slowly it seemed, **"The world is dying without Jesus, and all the church is doing is singing songs."** That really confused me. "But Lord," I said, "it's worship of you. Doesn't worship please you? Isn't worship important in the spiritual battles that lie before us?" I finished my trip in relative silence. I was sure that those words were from God, but I couldn't understand why God would ever say such a thing. Those words simmered in the back of my mind for days. And I wondered. How could God be displeased by worship?

New Brand of Idolatry

About a week later, I was watching a preacher on T.V. talk about bibliolatry, which he described as the worship of the Bible. He was referring to the attitude of a person who deeply reveres the book, but who fails to perceive or practice its message. Such an individual would never place the T.V. Guide on top of the Bible, nor would he permit dust to collect on its sacred cover or its holy pages. At the same time, neither would he open its cover or turn its pages in order to read it. The Bible becomes an idol in such a home, sitting day after day in a position of honor and reverence—unread. Like the evangelist I was watching, I believe that the bible is the infallible, inspired Word of God. However, what is important about the Bible is what God says to us in it. The object itself is not sacred; only what God says to us through it is. For instance, if I dropped my Bible in a mud puddle, I'd probably throw it away and buy a new one. That wouldn't anger God because we don't worship the Bible, we worship the God of the Bible.

As I watched that preacher talk about bibliolatry, the Holy Spirit reminded me of the experience I had driving my car. He said one word: worshipolatry. All the pieces began fitting together in my mind, and it all started to make sense. The world is dying without Jesus, and all the church is doing is singing songs. It's not that singing is wrong. What God was saying to me was that we have gone from worshipping Him to worshipping worship.

I gradually began to perceive things from God's perspective. Our young people are doing drugs. They dance and rock and roll as well as any of their peers who have never been in a church. Their parents are self-absorbed social drinkers who are more concerned with a new house or a new car than they are about their delinquent children or their own relationship with God. Our ministers are full of lust and are falling from the ministry in record numbers. And in the midst of this hellish onslaught, all we are doing is singing.

The Church of Jesus Christ in America is suffering from a severe spiritual malady. We are scarcely committed to God any more, and to make matters worse, we have determined to ignore that fact. We have closed our eyes to our lack of commitment because we don't want to have to look it in the face. We sin, but we do not repent. We don't even admit that what we have done is in fact sin at all. We avoid the unpleasantness of sin and the uncomfortable feelings we get when we consider our commitment to the Lord. We completely bypass these undesirable elements and move on to worship. It allows us to feel good about God, even though our relationship with Him is ailing. That is not the kind of worship God seeks.

Proper Worship: Truth

But an hour is coming, and now is, when the true worshipers shall worship the Father in spirit and truth; for such people the Father seeks to be His worshipers. God is spirit; and those who worship Him must worship in spirit and truth (John 4:23,24).

Jesus said that the true worshipers (indicating there are false worshipers) come to God not only in Spirit but also in truth. They deal with the truth of their relationship with God. They don't close their eyes to matters of commitment. They don't hem and haw about their sin. They're truthful about it, acknowledge it for what it is, and they repent. That's at the core of worship. It goes beyond just getting caught up in the moment, which is what often happens to us. After all, singing and worshipping appeals to our flesh. We can't help it; it just makes us feel good. Unfortunately, we tend to feel that the most proper worship is the worship that makes us feel best. We like that spiritual euphoria we get from worship, and soon enough, we find ourselves worshipping just for the good feelings we get. Worship gives us fulfillment, joy, and peace—all feelings coveted by man throughout history. Since worship gives us so much, we love it and look forward to it. but that's just the problem: we look forward to it, not to God. We find ourselves worshipping our own worship, instead of worshipping God. And according to Jesus, the only proper worship is based on truth; that is, on a pure, open relationship with God.

Proper Worship: Sacrifice

So it came about in the course of time that Cain brought an offering to the Lord of the fruit of the ground...but for Cain and his offering, the Lord had no regard. So Cain became very angry and his countenance fell (Gen. 4:3,5).

Cain sought to worship God by bringing Him an offering. However, God could not accept Cain's worship because his offering contained no blood sacrifice. In that dispensation of God's grace, the only acceptable sacrifice was a blood sacrifice, and that's not what he offered. Because of the very nature of God, He could not accept anything that did not have a blood sacrifice because the blood represented death or repentance. Repentance is that of dying to self.

Although we are in a different dispensation of God's grace, true worship still comes only through sacrifice. The sacrifice God seeks today is prayer. Prayer represents the death of self which will ultimately lead to repentance. Therefore, we cannot truly worship a God we do not pray to. Without a prayer life our offering of worship is as unacceptable to God as Cain's was.

Proper Worship: Reverence

> But as for me, by Thine abundant lovingkindness
> I will enter Thy house, At Thy Holy Temple I bow
> in reverence for Thee (Psa. 5:7).

When the Psalmist went to worship, bowing before God in the Temple, he did so in reverence, which is another crucial aspect of worship. He realized who God was. It was God who gave him his breath and fashioned mankind from the clay of the earth. Nothing existed until God created it, and at His command, all the universe sprang into existence. Because He willed it, light and life devoured the darkness and emptiness of the void. This was the God he bowed before, a holy God who knew no sin, no impurity: the one, true, perfect God. In great fear and trembling, the Psalmist, a mere fragile man, entered the presence of Almighty God to worship.

We have lost this sense of reverence for God. In spite of all our achievements, all our technological advancements, that technologically simple Bronze Age man, the Psalmist, possessed a treasure beyond measure: he possessed a reverence for God. Today we worship God with a cavalier attitude, concentrating more on the pleasure of worship than on the Lord. We get swept up in the joy of worship and forget who we're worshipping. Too frequently, we sing lacking the awe and respect which God should be accorded. And why is this?

> You hypocrites, rightly did Isaiah prophesy of you saying, 'This people honors Me with their lips, but their heart is far away from Me. But in vain do they worship Me, teaching as their doctrines the precepts of men.' " And he called to

134

Himself the multitude and said to them, "Hear and understand. Not what enters into the mouth defiles the man, but what proceeds out of the man, this defiles the man (Matt. 15:7-11).

Jesus told the Pharisees and scribes that what comes out of a man's mouth defiles him, for what a man speaks comes from his heart. The significance of this is it comes directly after saying, 'This people honors Me with their lips, but their heart is far from me.' If a man's heart is far away from God it indicates prayerlessness. It's a heart that does not pursue intimacy with God. Therefore, his mouth speaks evil, even though he may be worshipping at the time. If a man's heart is full of goodness, then his mouth speaks goodness. Our deficient worship is a result of the deficiencies in our hearts, and that is where God looks. He doesn't waste time with our words. Our words might be the inspired lyrics of a great hymn composed by one of the Wesleys, but if our life is prayless it is false worship. That's why God peers directly into our hearts when we offer up praises to Him.

Let me make it clear that I am not opposing worship. I'm just opposing worshipolatry, the false worship that has infiltrated our ranks. I am only against worshipping just for the sake of the peace and enjoyment it brings. I am only against worshipping when the worshiper is not allowing God to deal with the sin in his life. The worship I oppose is a false worship which lacks truth and reverence for God, having instead only reverence for the act of worship itself. It is exactly the kind of worship that will cause us to lose the spiritual battles ahead of us.

Spiritual Warfare

Spiritual warfare is not like physical warfare. In physical warfare the goal is to destroy your enemy. But in spiritual warfare, our goal is different. We have no hope of destroying Satan and his associates. The Bible makes this quite clear. What's more, we don't even have to try to defeat him. Satan is a defeated foe already. According to Hebrews 2:14, Jesus defeated the one who had the power of death.

To understand our goal in spiritual warfare, we have to understand Satan, who is still alive and still working just as actively as he was in Jesus' time. He is concocting a plot to destroy God, which he will try to accomplish at the battle of Armagedon. As we all know, Satan can't destroy God, or even come close to it. In that sense, he is already defeated. Since God is omnipotent, the enemy cannot do anything to physically harm Him. However, if he can get us to reject God's love, God will be hurt. The more he can lure us away from God and into his realm the more victorious he is.

This clarifies matters a great deal for us. Our enemy wants to draw us away from God. Therefore, our goal must be to draw closer to God. Spiritual warefare is primarily Satan opposing the development of Christ's character in us. If you want to truly confront the enemy, try to develop your personal prayer life. The more your life glorifies God, the more ineffective Satan is in this world. Anyone familiar with military strategy will quickly recognize that this situation means that we are on the defensive. I know a lot of Christians get charged up and excited and announce that they are on the offensive for God, but there is frankly no way we can be on the offensive. There is nothing we can do to Satan in an offensive sense. That's simply the way God has ordained things to be. However, we can defeat Satan's offensive attacks on mankind by glorifying Christ. Remember the war we're in was started by Satan for one reason: he doesn't want each of us to glorify Christ. We have the life of Christ. The enemy is trying to steal that life from us and keep it from others. Satan is mounting the offensive attack. All we have to do is protect what we already have: the life of Christ. If we do that, we will always be able to share it with others. Therefore, to worship God while still deeply involved in the world is false worship. We cannot identify in any way with the enemy and come to God in truth.

In our battle, worship is very important because it is the very act of glorifying God. However, the only worship of any value is the sort we've discussed so far: proper worship. That's worship in truth, in reverence and in sacrifice (prayer). To be involved in the world, which is being led astray by Satan, is to be identified with the enemy.

Excessive worship is a severe threat to the spirit of repentance. This truth was demonstrated clearly at the revival on Azusa Street during the first years of the twentieth century. With that revival came much worship. In the middle of one of the services, Frank Bartleman, the man in charge, stood up and said, "We must stop worshipping. We are worshipping so much that we are losing our spirit of conviction."

I thought that was very interesting. How could you ever worship too much? Then God began to deal with me on this whole concept of worshipolatry. You see, true worship, worship in the spirit of God, works in conjunction with repentance or truth. If we lose our spirit of repentance or conviction our worship of God will become false.

Yet I cannot overemphasize the power of true worship. It gets things done in the heavenly realm that nothing else can. That being the case, it would seem the more we worship the more God would be pleased. However, God isn't interested in doing things without using us. Consider this: what is standing in God's way from completely annihilating Satan? Absolutely nothing.

When you compare strength for strength, God could do it. However, God annihilates no one, not even Satan. We are all eternal beings. Satan will live forever in torment just as all non-believers will. God will ultimately remove him from the face of the earth but not annihilate him. Today God is more interested in us becoming like His Son than He is in anything else, and if it weren't for sin and the enemy, we probably wouldn't care anything about becoming like His Son. We probably wouldn't seek God at all. Seeing our enemy keeps us praying.

Pastor Cho, from Seoul, Korea, says the reason he and his people have experienced continual revival in Korea is because they have never lost sight of the enemy. Prayer Mountain is just thirty miles from the DMZ. They have Communist guns trained on their country. They can see their enemy, and that encourages them to cry out to their God.

In America we don't have an immediate human enemy as Korea does. But we have an even more powerful and more dangerous spiritual one, and we have lost sight of that enemy. In fact, we have embraced it. We have joined ranks with it. It's called worldliness. If you don't believe it has deceived us, just try to take it away from us. We will fight to the death for comfort - while character is not pursued at all.

Our Two Spiritual Garments

I once heard Rev. Bob Phillips, discuss the two spiritual garments we are to wear. One is the garment of praise the other the garment of sackcloth.

To grant those who mourn in Zion, Giving them garland instead of ashes, The oil of gladness instead of mourning, The garment of praise instead of a spirit of fainting. So they will be called oaks of

righteousness, The planing of the Lord, that He
may be glorified (Isa. 6:3).

Isaiah, under the inspiration of the Lord, wrote about
one of our spiritual garments, the garment of praise. It is
undoubtedly our favorite of the two. We put it on when
we are depressed or under great stress. It gives us great
relief and peace. It dispels any heaviness or depression. I
alluded to this earlier by mentioning that worship makes
us feel good. When we worship, we put on the garment of
praise.

The other spiritual garment, sackcloth, is far less
appealing. In the scriptures, God's people wore this garment as a sign of repentance. It was made of a very
uncomfortable material similar to burlap, the only difference being that it was less comfortable to wear than
burlap. The best thing you could say about sackcloth in
terms of comfort is that it was more comfortable than
sandpaper, but that's about it. Sackcloth was usually
accompanied by ashes as someone mourned his sin and
sought God.

In God's Word, the sackcloth was always to be put on
before the garment of praise. Mourning and repentance
always came first. God's people couldn't rejoice until
their problems with sin were taken care of. Please understand I am not placing these garments in the context of
receiving salvation. I'm not saying you need to wear
sackcloth in order to be saved, nor am I implying that you
aren't saved if you didn't wear sackcloth and ashes first.
I believe if you are in Christ, there is nothing more you can
do to gain salvation because you already have your
salvation as a gift of God. I am speaking in the context of
God's blood-bought redeemed Church living holy and
honorable lives before Him.

As saved, sanctified believers, we have involved
ourselves in things that we should have nothing to do

with. The Church is bloated with corruption.

Marketing has replaced miracles. By dipping into the world, we have learned how to con, cajole and trick congregations into donating to our ministries. We guarantee them that it really won't cost them anything to give because God will always return their donation ten fold (again despising sacrifice and denying that God would ask us to sacrifice). We smugly time our appeal for money so that we ask the congregation at the point when they are most likely to be wooed by us into giving. Fast talking and artfully designed pleas have replaced the moving of the Spirit to cause people to donate.

As a Church, we need to repent. But we won't. There is very little sense of, or sorrow over, the sin found in the Church. We have allied ourselves with the enemy, foolishly believing we can borrow his methods to reach God's ends. In the midst of this lack of repentance, we want to worship our troubles away. We sing until we feel at peace. We worship until we feel like we have put enough distance between us and the unpleasant thought of our hard, unrepentant hearts. We praise until we feel good. We worship, worship, worship. And then we worship some more. We may worship in Spirit, but we don't worship in truth, for we ignore the truth of our spiritual uncleanness in our worship. We become false worshipers. We honor the one, true, holy God with our lips, but our hearts are far from Him. Therefore, we worship in vain.

A prayerless church cannot be brought to repentance. The garment of sackcloth represents our prayer life, it rubs us the wrong way, it reminds us of our continual need to let God search our hearts. Currently, the church has the garment of praise on instead of sackcloth and subsequently cannot sense her need for repentance. The church must take off the garment of praise in order to put on sackcloth. This does not mean we should stop worshiping, but rather that we must start praying.

> Therefore in that day the Lord God of hosts, called
> you to weeping, to wailing, To shaving the head,
> and to wearing sackcloth. Instead, there is gaiety
> and gladness, Killing of cattle and slaughtering of
> sheep, Eating of meat and drinking of wine; 'Let
> us eat and drink for tomorrow we may die' (Isa.
> 22:12,13).

Isaiah was preaching to a people who had forgotten
their God. They had indulged their carnal desires without
remorse, satisfying every whim they possibly could. God
called them to repentance, to return to Him once again.
But they had no room in their hearts for Him. He called
them to repentance, to mourning over their sin in sackcloth and ashes and then to turn from their wicked ways.
But God's people wanted no part of wearing sackcloth,
the garment that would make them uncomfortable and
deny their insatiable lust for pleasure. They just wanted
to have a good time, and they wanted to do it without
their God. Those people were a lot like we are. God has
called us to put on sackcloth, but we won't take off the
garment of praise. We revel in our hollow worship, which
is no more true worship than that of God's people in
Isaiah's day. Then, as now, God's people are worshipping
this life. They are using praise and worship to get from
God what they want in life. God is saying, "Repent, of the
sin you have discovered in your ranks," but all we are
doing is enjoying life, eating and drinking, happy that it's
not us that got caught in sin.

Jehoshaphat

Jehoshaphat was a godly man, one of the few kings of
Judah who was. The scriptures tell us that "the Lord was

with Jehoshaphat because he followed the example of his father David's earlier days and did not seek the Baals, but sought the God of his father, following His command- ments..." (2 Chronicles 17:3, 4). The Bible goes so far as to compare him with King David, and not only that, but it compares him to David in his earlier days, in his best days. Jehoshaphat was favorably likened to the best of the best. He sought after God, even though generations of kings before him worshipped false gods. He was a man who stood for God at an ungodly time, when it was least expected of him. Like David he was a man after God's own heart. Maybe that is what makes this portion of his life especially sad.

> Now Jehoshaphat had great riches and honor; and he allied himself by marriage with Ahab (2 Chron. 18:1).

After God rewarded his faithfulness, giving him riches and honor, Jehoshaphat made a serious mistake by making an alliance with one of the most wicked monarchs to ever rule in the promised land. God referred to King Ahab as "an Asheroth," which was an idol (2 Chronicles 19:3). Ashera was a Phoenician goddess embraced by the Isra- elites, over whom Ahab was king. More specifically, Ashera was a fertility goddess. This meant that worship- ping Ashera would involve great sexual excess and immorality. The idolatrous Israelites were giving them- selves over, mind, heart and spirit, to the lusts of their flesh. By calling him an Asheroth, God was saying that Ahab was the quintessence of Israel's idolatry and de- pravity. Jehoshaphat made the grave mistake of believing that he could ally himself with God's enemies.

It's easy for us to look back and say, "That certainly was foolish of Jehoshaphat. He knew God. He should have realized his alliance with Ahab would lead only to hardship." We all have twenty-twenty hindsight. In our present age, however, we do not perceive spiritual truth with such crystal clarity either. We say it was obvious Jehoshaphat's alliance with the enemy was certain disaster, yet we see nothing wrong when we ally ourselves with our enemy. We cannot join sides with Satan to fight Satan. Yet that is what is happening if we are trying to engage in warfare prayer while living with a known sin in our lives. If we have taken sides with sin, then we have opened ourselves to deception. I have always maintained that without an intimate relationship with God through prayer, we lose discernment, which is the heart of the war. We need to recognize the schemes of Satan. King Jehoshaphat lost his ability to do that when he lost his discernment. And he walked right into a spiritual trap.

> And Ahab king of Israel said to Jehoshaphat king of Judah, "Will you go with me against Ramoth-gilead?" And he said to him, "I am as you are, and my people as your people, and we will be with you in the battle" (2 Chron. 18:3).

Almost blind for lack of discernment, Jehoshaphat staggered into the first deception: "We are just like you, we will be with you in the battle." This statement by Ahab was the first in a series of deceptions.

> Moreover, Jehoshaphat said to the king of Israel, "Please inquire first for the word of the Lord" (2 Chron. 18:4).

Jehoshaphat wasn't completely lost, though. He was flirting with the world, but he still knew in his heart that Jehovah was God of heaven and earth. He wanted to know what He had to say about this plan of King Ahabs.

Then the King of Israel assembled the prophets, four hundred men, and said to them, "Shall we go against Ramoth-gilead to battle, or shall I refrain?" And they said, "Go up, for God will give it into the hand of the king." But Jehoshaphat said, "Is there not yet a prophet of the Lord here that we may inquire of him?" (2 Chron. 18:5,6).

Jehoshaphat knew what was going on in Israel, how the people had turned their backs on God. He wasn't quite convinced that he was going to be blessed in his alliance with Ahab. He wanted to hear it from one of Jehovah's prophets, not just from Ahab's yes-man prophets.

And the king of Israel said to Jehoshaphat, "There is yet one man by whom we may inquire of the Lord, but I hate him, for he never prophesies good concerning me but always evil. He is Micaiah, son of Imla" (2 Chron. 18:7).

In spite of (or perhaps because of) Israel's sin, there was still a true prophet in the land. However, as one might expect, his message was being rejected. The people, especially King Ahab, wanted Micaiah to tell them that it was the best of times, and that things were only getting better. Of course, that wasn't Micaiah's style. He was a man of God, and he would speak only what the Lord told him to do. So it comes as no surprise that when Ahab inquired of him, Micaiah said that Ahab was not shepherding his people and that he would die if he went into battle. Then the prophet gives us a glimpse into the spiritual realm.

And Micaiah said, "Therefore hear the word of the Lord, I saw the Lord sitting on His throne, and all the host of heaven standing on His right and on His left. And the Lord said, 'Who will entice Ahab, king of Israel to go up and fall at Ramoth-gilead?' And one said this while another said that. Then a spirit came forward and stood before the Lord and said, 'I will entice him.' And the Lord said to him, 'How?' And he said, 'I will go and be a deceiving spirit in the mouth of all his prophets.' Then he said, 'You are to entice him and prevail also, go and do so.' Now therefore, the Lord has put a deceiving spirit in the mouth of your prophets; for the Lord has proclaimed disaster against you" (2 Chron. 18:18-21).

When Ahab's prophets told the king that he would have nothing but success if he went to war, they weren't just making it up. They were speaking what they had perceived in the spiritual realm. The false prophets weren't in touch with demons, either. Quite the contrary, Ahab's charlatans were in communication with the hosts of heaven, God's forces working as deceptive spirits. And those angelic spirits were very successful. Not only was Ahab deceived, but so was Jehoshaphat, a man after God's own heart. You see when we side with the enemy, when we become worldly, we open ourselves to great deception. We can be just as deceived as Jehoshaphat was if we flirt with the world. We must understand that Jehoshaphat was looking for truth. He wanted to know what God had to say. However, when he heard the true prophet he did not heed his words because he had willfully allied himself with Ahab. He'd lost his discernment. Isn't it interesting that today a "prophetic" movement has been born out of such a worldly church. A church knowingly allied with the world cannot possibly be speaking God's true words. Not much has changed from then to now. The false prophets are saying, "All things are fine just keep on keeping on." While the more accurate prophetic word is "repent". Todays church has rejected the prophetic message of repentance and is clinging to the majority of the current false prophet's message of peace and tranquility.

Being deceived as he was, Jehoshaphat went into battle just as he and Ahab had planned to. The battle was a disaster. The two Jewish kings suffered a staggering defeat, and Ahab was killed in the battle, just as it was prophesied he would.

Jehoshaphat returned home after the trouncing he and his men suffered. Not long after his return, the prophet Jehu came out to give King Jehoshaphat a Word from God.

> And Jehu the son of Hanani the seer went out to meet him and said to King Jehoshaphat, "Should you help the wicked and love those who hate the Lord and so bring wrath on yourself from the Lord?" (2 Chron. 19:2).

Like all of God's prophets in the Old Testament, Jehu got right to the heart of the matter. The king had been helping the wicked and loving those who hated the Lord and, in so doing, he was inviting God's wrath upon him. Loving the world naturally brings God's wrath upon us, just as surely as it brings deception upon us. I believe the Church's current love of pleasure and the things of this world has deceived us. We will not listen to the watchmen.

But Jehoshaphat realized that he had sinned by loving and involving himself with the world. He knew doing that deceived him, and that God's wrath would surely follow if he did not repent. So he did repent and put on sackcloth as a sign of his repentance. Then he began to live in harmony with His God.

Then one day, it was reported to him that foreigners in ships from far off were preparing to launch an invasion against him and his people. He didn't want it, but he got it: war. But he wasn't going to handle it the same way he handled the situation with Ahab; he wouldn't immediately put on the garment of praise. Instead, he put on sackcloth and turned his attention and that of the whole nation to seeking their God. He proclaimed a fast throughout all Judah.

And all Judah was standing before the Lord, with their infants, their wives, and their children. Then in the midst of the assembly the Spirit of the Lord came upon Jahaziel...and he said, "Listen, all Judah and the inhabitants of Jerusalem and King Jehoshaphat: thus says the Lord to you, `Do not fear or be dismayed because of this great multitude, for the battle is not yours but God's. You need not fight in this battle; station yourselves, stand and see the salvation of the Lord on your behalf, O Judah and Jerusalem, do not fear or be dismayed; tomorrow go out to face them for the Lord is with you" (2 Chron. 20:12-17).

All this time they have had the sackcloth on. They were repenting, fasting and seeking God. Then they entered into a battle. But it wasn't a typical battle. Just as God had told them, it was a spiritual battle, and they didn't even need to fight it. Yet they did prepare, though not the way any people of that era ever prepared for a battle.

And when he had consulted with the people, he appointed those who sang to the Lord and those who praised Him in holy attire as they went out before the army and said, "Give thanks to the

Lord, for His lovingkindness is everlasting." And when they began singing and praising, the Lord set ambushes against the sons of Ammon, Moab, and Mount Seir, who had come against Judah; so they were routed. For the sons of Ammon and Moab rose up against the inhabitants of Mount Seir destroying them completely, and when they had finished with the inhabitants of Seir, they helped to destroy one another. When Judah came to the lookout of the wilderness, they looked toward the multitude; and behold, they were corpses lying on the ground, and no one had escaped" (2 Chron. 20:21-22).

Worship is powerful, it confuses the enemy, and no where has that fact been demonstrated more clearly than in that battle. Satan is playing for keeps. He is out to kill and destroy. If he can't get to us, He'll turn on his own followers. True worship will so confuse the enemy that he will destroy his own followers.

In our spiritual warfare, God uses our worship to accomplish very special purposes. He uses worship to get His work done in the world. Prayer, on the other hand, is what God uses to get work done in us. Worship changes the world. Prayer changes us. But in order for this to happen, the garment of praise must go on after the sackcloth. If we reverse that, putting on the garment of praise first, we never bring ourselves to repentance, we ensnare ourselves in a worship of worship, rather than a worship of the one true God.

Prayer, Preaching and Praise

There is a certain pattern most churches follow in their worship services. They begin by singing choruses and hymns. Then the minister brings his message to the congregation, which is followed by a period of prayer. The pattern is praise, preaching, prayer. But that's not the pattern I see in Scripture and in the lives of those who are being greatly used by God. In fact, it's exactly the opposite. In Scripture, I see prayer first, followed by preaching, then praise. Take a look back at Jehoshaphat. He began with prayer, that is, communication with God. He sought God and repented of his sin. He fasted. That is God working in us.

Then he was instructed to take his position at the battle front. This was where the preaching of God's Word came in: it prepares us for the battle, it equips us for the fighting we will face. After all, the Bible is the Sword of the Spirit. But that's not all it is. It's that and more. It is also what we station ourselves upon in battle. It allows us to stand firm without slipping. It gives us stability. Once God has worked in us and equipped us through His Word, we are ready for battle—then we enter into worship.

This is the pattern God has worked into my life. I must stress that God worked it into my life; I wasn't born with this blueprint. I started off as many Christians do. The only thing I felt was important was the Word of God. I was only half right. The Word of God is important, but it is not the only thing that is important. However, at the time, I was convinced that the Word of God was my only resource. I went to Bible college to study the Word. I memorized it. I committed to memory over fifty chapter of Scripture. I memorized half of Isaiah, and some of the Pauline Epistles. Even with all that, I was very ineffective as a minister. I realized that there must be more for me spiritually than the Word of God. Finally I began to respond to God concerning prayer. I began to give myself to prayer. I found myself entering into spiritual warfare, really for the first time.

I remember being in prayer one night around midnight in the living room of our apartment. Suddenly a very cold chill gnawed through my body. Temperatures well below zero were not uncommon in the winter. But this was something different. It instantly froze me right down to the core of my being. With that was a tremendous presence of evil. It was as if a black mist had suddenly settled on our apartment and was swirling around. As I turned around, I saw two figures standing in the corner of the room. I had never seen beings like that before, at least not in real life. However, they looked very much like drawings of the fictional grim reaper. They were engulfed in big black cloaks that stretched all the way down to the floor. They wore hoods that drooped a little in front of their faces, obscuring whatever was beneath those hoods in shadows. The sight of them wasn't what was most terrifying. What was the worst was the hideous sense of malevolence that streamed from them. I quickly realized I was at a battle front.

I continued to pray and praise for a long time until they had left the room. When they left my room, they went to my wife, who was sleeping. I had a sudden sense that they were going to attack her physically with some type of stomach pain. I went back to prayer, and for the next twenty minutes I battled with that. The next day, as I was praying about that, God seemed to impress me with the importance of that battle in my life. It was a point of great decision in my life. As I was praying, I realized that the only way to avoid confronting Satan was to stop praying. I had a choice to make. I could either stop praying so that I wouldn't ever have this uncomfortable experience again, or I could forge on ahead, come what may, and entrust myself to God. I chose to stick with God and continue praying. It was a very important point of decision for me. I was putting on the sackcloth in my life. God had been dealing with me for several weeks about my relationship with Him. I was experiencing something with Him that I had never experienced before. Prayer was changing me. It was changing my worship of Him. It was changing my effectiveness for Him, and that just made Satan angry.

God was rearranging the order of my life. It was to be prayer first (intimacy with Him), the Word second (knowledge of Him), and then worship (spiritual warfare). Once I began to pray, everything else fell in order. The scriptures that I had memorized began to make sense to me; I gained insight that I had never had before. In a more powerful sense than I had ever thought possible, God's Word became my sword. What's more, worship took on a whole new perspective. I began to worship God. I mean really worship God. My heart would ache for God. I wanted God and nothing else. Worship was no longer rote. It was no longer something I did in hopes that I could con God into doing something.

My ministry began to take on a new dimension, too. I was on staff at a church as the minister of prayer. We were following the typical pattern of praise, preaching, and prayer. However, after some time, prayer became the primary focus of the church, not just something we did at the end of a service. We began Morning Manna, a morning prayer meeting that met every week day. We had an all-night prayer meeting once a month. We had sermon intercessors before and even during the services. Our prayer room was open for (and doing) business the whole day.

One day I was driving from Milwaukee to Kenosha on I-94. As I approached Kenosha, in the spirit I saw a black evil cloud hovering over our city. Suddenly there appeared in the middle of it an opening like the eye of a hurricane, directly over our city. From that point on, the gospel had tremendous freedom in our city. We went from growing less than 100 people a year to over 400 in one year. After prayer took it's proper place in the order of things, our worship of God broke through the spiritual bondage of our city, which allowed the Word of God to have a much greater effect than it ever had in the past.

Worship has become such a powerful thing in our church that the music ministry is one of the most effective soul-winning efforts we have. We've also found that prayer enhanced every other ministry in the church. Because we set our faces to seek our God, everything else fell into its proper place.

Worship is most powerful. However, its not just worship that does it—it's worship of our God. It's coming to Him not only in Spirit but also in truth.

TEN

VIOLENT MEN

The army of God moves out on its knees.
—Anonymous

The swaggering pharisees would have been scarcely clad if they were clothed only in their humility. They were so arrogant that they taught the people that they were the only ones who would hold a place of esteem in heaven because only they were good enough. The people were told that they would have to measure up to the righteousness and piety of the pharisees. But Jesus challenged their haughty teachings.

> Truly I say to you, among those who are born of women, there has not arisen anyone greater than John the Baptist. Yet he who is least in the kingdom of heaven is greater than he (Matt. 11:11).

Jesus was implying that because no one was greater

than John the Baptist, the pharisees were not greater than John, either. That was radical teaching: John the Baptist was greater than the pharisees. (To say that John the Baptist was even as great as the pharisees would have been radical). Then He went on to challenge another of the pharisees' false doctrines.

> And from the days of John the Baptist until now the kingdom of heaven suffers violence, and violent men take it by force (Matt. 11:12).

The pharisees taught that tax collectors and heathens really had no right to enter heaven at all. Christ countered that teaching by telling the multitudes that they could literally take heaven by force. They could enter the kingdom of heaven ahead of all these respected, educated doctors who had been claiming the kingdom of heaven for themselves. Anyone who was full of holy zeal and earnestness could seize at once the mercy of the gospel, and so take the kingdom of God as by force.

That teaching remains just as true today. Any person who is going to take possession of the kingdom of righteousness, peace and joy must be in earnest. All hell will oppose him every step of the way. If a man is not absolutely determined to give up on his sin, then obviously he is going to perish. There is a tremendous battle that is taking place over the souls of men. If we could have seen what took place in the heavenlies when each of us gave his life to Christ, we would see a graphic illustration of this point. Your salvation came through violence. But once you accepted Christ, your victory came and the battle for your soul was won.

A Spiritual Battle

We are no longer in a battle for our soul. While Satan

is still out to deceive us, nothing can separate us from the love of Christ. We can still choose to turn our backs on God, but nothing and no one, not even Satan and all his demonic cohorts, can make that decision for us. But as soon as we obtain eternal life, we enter into another battle: the battle for the souls of other men. Both the forces of God and the forces of Satan are battling for souls.

When we hear about battle, we immediately think of the American Civil War, World War II or the Vietnam War. Our battle is just as fierce (if not more fierce) than any of these battles that have been seen by human eyes. Our battle requires powerful men just as every physical war has. But there's one great difference between the wars we have seen in movies or read about in books: this one is spiritual. That means it rages around us everyday, but it it unseen by the human eye. Yet it is the most important war of all time. The outcome of this battle will determine where a man will spend eternity, making it the greatest, most important battle he will ever face.

With so much at stake, we need believers who know how to do battle, men who will never give up, men who will give their lives for the sake of others. Jesus said that we need violent men. However, the violence He referred to is not violence of the type that plagues our society (i.e., that of doing harm to one another). The Greek word that we translate "violent" is best used to describe one who is forceful and unrelenting—just as forceful and unrelenting as our enemy in the battle that lies before us.

It's also important for us to realize that Satan is unlike any threat or enemy we will ever face on this earth. He never gives up his fight against God's people. Lucifer doesn't give his enemy days off for national holidays, and he doesn't take coffee breaks. He is relentless. He never stops not even to catch his breath. I really came to grasp the depth of his persistence one day when I was walking by Lake Michigan, which is just a block from my home in

Kenosha, Wisconsin. Being one of the Great Lakes, it is the closest thing to an ocean you'll ever see without actually seeing an ocean. You certainly can't see to the other side. The waves lap at the shore day and night. Sometimes they pound with greater force than at other times, but they never stop. Over a long period of time, the most gentle waves are able to wear down solid rock because of their consistency. Our adversary, the Devil, is just as relentless. He is always trying to wear down the saints.

God's Strength, Not Ours

Because Satan is so tenacious, God's men must be equally so. Satan is forceful, so God's warriors must be just as forceful. However, we are not to depend on physical force because our battle is not a physical one. It is a spiritual battle and we are to depend on God's force.

> Finally, my brethren, be strong in the Lord and in the power of His might (Eph. 6:10).

We are to become strong in the Lord. That is our objective. We want the power of His might, not the power of our own might. It is not our strength that we use in a spiritual battle. It is God's strength, so any of us, regardless of our stature or our age, can become a powerhouse spiritually. Even though that sounds great, it is a stumbling block to many.

When we think of battles, we often dream of musclemen forcing their way through incredible barriers despite impossible odds, and we make the mistake of applying this to our spiritual battle. We think that if we can grit our teeth, and if we can get angry enough and indignant enough, then our intensity can force Satan out. That's a serious error because it is a physical approach to a spiritual battle. We need to be reminded that although we

156

walk in the flesh, we do not war according to the flesh. The weapons of our spiritual warfare are mighty only through God. Those weapons are the ones that pull down strongholds and cast down imagination.

So how do we become forceful in God's strength? It's simple once we understand that force is born of rest. That's not what we expect. Rest and force seem mutually exclusive, yet we must rest in the Lord to become forceful spiritually.

> Those who wait for the Lord will gain new strength. They will mount up with wings like eagles. They will run and not get tired. They will walk and not become weary (Isa. 40:31).

When this verse speaks about waiting for God, it doesn't mean that we are to sit around twiddling our thumbs. This word "wait" in the Hebrew language implies a very close relationship. In the context of this verse, it's like being braided to God, or like having both hands gripped onto God, so that we are so firmly attached to God that when He moves, we have to move along with Him. That's how we are to rest in the Lord.

We often associate resting with being lax and doing nothing. But resting in God means developing a closeness to Him, being knitted together with the Lord. We could translate this verse, "They who are braided to God will gain new strength."

We are to become unrelenting, fierce warriors in the battle for souls, but that sounds tiring. However, if we attempt to become fierce, unrelenting warriors without resting in the Lord, we will become quickly exhausted and will probably give up. We must remember that the only way we will have enough strength to make it through the battle is by resting in God, for then He will give us supernatural strength.

Consistency Builds Strength

When I was in college, I had a friend, Roger, who was a jogging enthusiast. He jogged about ten miles every day. I could never understand how he could do it. It must have been genetics because I tried doing the same thing on three separate occasions, and I couldn't even make it a mile. Roger's secret was really no secret at all: it was consistency. He had been jogging for about three years when I met him. Because he did it very day, year in, year out, he gradually grew strong enough to run ten miles. Physical exercise builds physical strength—just as spiritual exercise builds spiritual strength.

If we are going to become forceful men and women of God, then we must become consistent in our prayer lives because spiritual exercise will produce spiritual strength. That's the only way. We won't gain strength by gritting our teeth, flexing our muscles and shouting threats at the enemy. Our spiritual strength will be directly proportional to our spiritual consistency.

I think we miss the point sometimes when we get all excited about the armor of God outlined in Paul's letter to the Ephesians. We put on the helmet of salvation, we put on the breastplate of righteousness, then we gird our loins for truth and get ready for the battle. And when we've strapped on the whole armor of God, we say we're going into the battle. But putting on the armor of God is only a step of preparation for the battle. We can't actually get into the battle without prayer. Because we as a Church tend not to pray much, we spend most of our time just getting ready for the battle without actually battling the enemy much at all. Without consistent prayer, we cannot do battle.

Consistency Changes the Pray-er

When I was saved, God changed me. He set me free from many bad habits that had become deeply entrenched in me over a number of years. However, there were some habits that He didn't set me free of. For years after I was saved, I struggled with them. As a young believer, I was very frustrated with these habits that still clung to me. I knew that God could set me free of these habits as easily as He had set me free of those other ones.

However, God, seemingly doesn't always set us free from all of our habits and weaknesses instantly. God wants to spend time with us and sometimes those foibles are the only things that keep us praying. If we pray about nothing else, we will at least pray about our problem. If we were instantly set free, we would stop praying. **Should God set us free from the only thing that is causing us to spend any time with Him?** God knows our heart and He knows if we are praying only to get something from Him. With that type of mentality towards prayer, you will always have struggles even though you pray much.

So can a person be set free from an old problem? Yes, but only when he makes the decision that prayer is going to be a big part of his life no matter what God does in response to his praying. He must decide that he is going to pray in order to develop a relationship with God, not just to get things from Him. Deliverance comes the moment God knows He has your heart. When you pray more for the sake of getting God rather than getting something from God, He can deliver you knowing that even though you no longer have the problem you will keep praying.

Many people are trying to find strength and deliverance through prayer, and they can't. There is no strength or deliverance in prayer. You can find strength and deliverance only in God. We must find our rest in Him alone. Prayer is just an avenue that leads to God, so we must pursue God, not prayer.

His Load Is Light

After Jesus explained the need for violent men who will be unrelenting in their fight against the enemy, he said something that seems contradictory.

My yoke is easy and my load is light (Matt. 11:30).

Earlier in the same chapter He said we must be unrelenting warriors because this battle will not end during our lifetimes. We mustn't stop praying when we win a victory here or when we win a skirmish there. We should never ask God to give us a victory so we can stop praying. This life is a continuous battle. This is the day of work. You can get to feel exhausted just thinking about a battle that lasts a lifetime, to say nothing of actually fighting in it. So how could He say, "My yoke is easy?"

His yoke is easy and His burden is light only through our consistency in prayer. If we persevere in prayer, we will truly know what it is to bear His burden and His yoke. But if we pray only during a crisis, then stop praying when the crisis has subsided, we will feel drained, and the next battle will make us even more fatigued and more weary.

When you pray only when you are staggering beneath the weight of a crisis, you get the idea that prayer is a difficult, exhausting thing to do. As a result, you will avoid prayer. It will hardly seem like a yoke that is easy or a burden that is light.

However, when you pray consistently every day, and then you face some kind of tragedy, you will be able to just add that matter to your daily prayer. You will have exercised regularly enough so that you have enough spiritual strength to face that challenge. You'll be like another friend of mine in college who studied every day, so that when exam time came, he had no need to study any more than he did at any other time.

The yoke of consistent prayer can be so light that other believers might think that you are uncaring. I remember when I received a phone call telling me that my mother found my dad unconscious on the bathroom floor, suffering from a bleeding ulcer. My mom called me and asked me to pray for him, so I did. I prayed for him longer than I usually did in my daily prayer time, and I was concerned for him. But I didn't alter my life because of this crisis. I simply added that issue to my daily prayer time. My consistency in prayer had made me so confident in God that I trusted Him. I knew that worry wouldn't help my dad. I knew that praying was the only thing I could do to help him. And I knew that praying was the most powerful thing I could ever do to help him in any situation.

The Humble Heart

Come to Me, all you that are weary and heavy-laden, and I will give you rest. Take my yoke upon you and learn from Me, for I am gentle and humble of heart, and you shall find rest for your soul (Matt. 11:28-29).

Jesus asks us to come and be with Him. It's a call to intimacy. Then He gives us rest, and that's what we need, because force is born of rest. Then He asks us to be gentle and humble of heart. But just before this, Jesus was talking about the need for forceful men of war. This confounds our human understanding of things. First, He says He wants forceful men, so we say, "Fine." We psyche ourselves up, imagine ourselves as some kind of spiritual powerhouse, and then practice snarling and sneering at Satan. But then Jesus turns around (or so it seems to us) and tells us to learn from Him for He is gentle and humble of heart. We can't imagine "forceful men" ever being gentle or humble of heart in the least.

This is so crucial because it teaches us that Christ works through us by means of developing His character in us. The more Christ-like we become, the more powerful we are in spiritual battle. We need that power that comes from Him. Our own power, our shouting and our determination are nothing to Satan. It doesn't matter how much we grit our teeth or how much we flex our muscles. Satan laughs at such exhibitions because they accomplish nothing. He and his forces can resist human strength forever. In fact, they can ignore it forever. But when we come to him in the power and authority of Jesus Christ, Satan has to flee.

Doing Things for God, or with God?

One of our greatest mistakes in spiritual warfare is our struggle to do things for God. He never asked us to do things for Him. Instead, He really wants us to do things with Him. He wants us to work by His side, so that we can say with Jesus, "I do only what I see my Father in heaven doing."

When we try to do something for God, we find ourselves searching for tools. What do we end up latching onto? Prayer and the Bible. We use them to help us do things for God. But prayer and the Bible were never designed to help us do work. They were given to us so that we could get to know God. They are here so that we can develop an intimate relationship with our Creator.

The worst result of misusing prayer and the Bible is that we eventually use them to manipulate God. We wave our Bibles at Him, then threaten Him that He'd better make sure that He holds true to every word of it. Instead of treasuring God's truths in our hearts and getting to know Him better, we end up shouting and stomping our feet like insufferably spoiled children.

But when we are doing things with God, we depend on His strength. As a result, we just naturally use prayer and God's Word to enhance and develop our relationship with Him. We study His Word for one reason: to get to know Him. We pray for one reason: to get to know Him. There's no manipulation, and there's no need for it. If we work with Him, not for Him, we won't succumb to spiritual burn-out because we won't be depending on our own strength, but on His.

There was a man who was driving down an old country road when he saw two oxen working in a field. They were wearing the traditional yoke, but one of them was very small while the other one was very large. The man stopped and asked the farmer why he would match such a large oxen with such a small one. The farmer replied, "The yoke keeps them together. Because of the size of the larger oxen, the younger one can do nothing but follow in his footsteps. All the weight of the work is resting on the shoulders of the large oxen."

Jesus wants us to be yoked with Him. Then he bears the weight of the work. That's why He wants us to take His yoke. It is easy and light. It will give us rest. Even in the midst of the battle we can gain strength—but only when we find our rest in Christ through daily prayer.

ELEVEN

PLAIN MEN OF GOD

You have to give men the biggest show on earth. If you can't you shouldn't bother giving them anything.
—P.T. Barnum

If Jesus were walking the earth today, He would be hard-pressed to compete with the modern, high-tech, polished evangelists of this age. Jesus did everything backwards, according to our standards today. First of all, even though He had twelve apostles, He didn't have even one public relations practitioner. If He had a good P.R. staff, there would have been no doubt about who He was. Why just look at all the opportunities He missed out on because He didn't have anyone to help Him take advantage of them!

Just consider the first ten chapters of John's gospel. Jesus turned water into wine (chapter 2), He revealed the sin of the woman at the well through a word of knowledge (chapter 4), He healed the nobleman's son (chapter 4), He caused a man to walk who hadn't walked in 38 years (chapter 5), He miraculously fed 5,000 men with a few fish and some bread (chapter 6), He walked on water (chapter 6), and He healed a man born blind (chapter 9).

Jesus obviously failed to advertise Himself properly because there were still skeptics asking who He was.

> The Jews therefore gathered around Him, and were saying to Him, "How long will you keep us in suspense? If you are the Christ, tell us plainly" (John 10:24).

After all these miracles, there were still people around Him saying, "Tell us plainly who you are." If Jesus was going to compete with a modern American evangelist, He'd have to start getting his ministry together. First He would have to organize and compile some promotional literature that would list all the miracles He had performed in great detail.

Then He would have to go to some graphics and design firm to have some sharp, professional posters designed—but not just any posters; each poster would be big enough to cover an entire wall! Each one would contain pictures of the miracles. He could have a shot of 5,000 happy people smiling and eating the bread and fish He miraculously multiplied. Then He could have a shot of the Holy Spirit descending in the form of a dove. At the bottom of the poster, there could be testimonials: "Behold, the Lamb of God who takes away the sin of the world!—John the Baptist," and "This is My beloved Son in whom I am well pleased!—God." (Jesus would have been the only evangelist who could have said God wrote His promotional material; the rest of us have to admit that we paid somebody else to do it).

Excuse Me; Is There a Plain Man of God in the House?

I was doing a seminar in a small Church in southern Minnesota, and the pastor of that Church and I were discussing the election of an important denominational office. The winner would be in charge of a district of 200 Churches that would include the one I was at. That pastor I was speaking to made a remark that spoke very deeply to my heart: "We need a plain man of God."

Nothing could probably be more true in the age we live in. The Church doesn't need entertaining preachers who can make us laugh but who can't speak with the anointing of God. We don't need slick showmen with flashy personalities. We don't need sophisticated singers who aim to entertain the masses but who care little about ministering to them. The Church needs plain men of God who will concentrate on God alone, men who will serve Him no matter who notices. We need men who will give at least as much time to the nurturing of the saints as they do to the styling of their hair.

John the Baptist

There came a man, sent from God, whose name was John. He came for a witness, that He might bear witness of the light, that all might believe through him. He was not the light, but came that he might bear witness to the light (John 1:6-8).

Poor John the Baptist. He really got a bad deal. There he was, sent from God, and what did he get? He got stuck wearing clothes made out of camel's hair. Think about his living accommodations; he didn't have any. He had to live outside in the wilderness. Consequently, he didn't have room service. In fact, he ate only what he could find out in the wilderness, things like wild honey and locusts. He didn't even have a catchy P.O. Box that was easy to memorize.

What did God think He was doing?

I can tell you what He was doing, but it might come as an unpleasant shock to some of us evangelists. God was sending a man to bear witness to the Light, but—and this is the shocking part—the man God sent was not the Light. The man sent by God was a plain man of God. He wasn't living for his own aggrandizement or comfort. John knew Jesus was coming as the Savior of the world, as the cleanser of sin, so John set his face like flint. He refused to accept any glory for himself. John's objective was to glorify Jesus and to make straight a path for His coming Lord. That selflessness confuses us. How could God use someone who cared so little for his own advancement?

Although it may seem like a paradox to us, God was able to use John because he cared so little about his own "career." His attitude made it easy for God to lift him up and give him a place in history. God actually placed John in a position where he was required to baptize the Son of God. And it didn't require networking with other preachers and playing political games with influential people. John just lived to fulfill God's will, and he trusted Him to bring it about.

Poor John. He lacked the sophistication and shrewdness to make something out of himself, in spite of all the obvious opportunities that had been set in front of him. He could have promoted himself as "the world's most anointed baptizer." On his promo table, he could have marketed wild honey and locusts, "the breakfast of champions and of the world's most anointed baptizer." He could have sold camel hair T-shirts, and real leather belts have always been in and good for a few bucks. This guy had it made. He could have finally struck it rich! No more "Grizzly Adams" lifestyle. He could start living like a "king's kid." He could have bought a condo on the outskirts of Jerusalem! No more living outside like some transient. He could have started eating delicacies fit for the table of Governor Pilate or of even Caesar himself! He could have had the best of everything, He could have stuck his audiences and fans with all the camel hair, and he could have bought the latest in fashionable Roman togas. He could have even picked up an imported Roman chariot. That would prove to everyone how much God loved him. He could have had so many drachmas, he couldn't spend them all. After all, that is obviously God's will for all of His servants, isn't it?

But then something went wrong. He finished the work God had given him by preparing the way for the Messiah, but you would think John could have retired to some nice little island in the Mediterranean, or something. John reached the zenith of his career, he baptized the very Son of God, and then he was thrown into jail because he preached God's ways of righteousness and holiness to the Jewish puppet-king, Herod. Just about the time his mailing list was at the point where he could expect God to perform financial miracles by the third week of every month, he was thrown in jail. In the end, he was beheaded on orders from King Herod.

In spite of all these apparent failures in John's life, he went down in history as a man sent by God. He was a plain man of God who accomplished exactly what God wanted him to accomplish. What more do we need to accomplish in this life?

Glorifying Who?

A friend of mine, an evangelist, came up to my wife, Lou Ann, and said, "If you're going to be the wife of an evangelist, you need a lot more hair than you have. You're also going to need more make-up. And where in the world is your jewelry?" He's a very good friend, and I had no doubt that he was only kidding. However, as Shakespeare once observed, the things said in jest are often most true. Many men would have said quite seriously what my friend said in jest. Men have always sought their own glory.

When I was a young Christian, a well-known singing group visited our church. I was still enjoying my "first love" state of mind. I was completely taken up with Jesus. God had completely transformed my life by renewing my mind. Because of that, I was surprised when the leader of the group asked us to applaud after each song. To me, that was the old way of thinking. That was the state of mind I had when I was in the world listening to performers who performed for their own exaltation. God had renewed my mind, and I struggled with an "anointed" singing group coveting the approval of men.

Unfortunately, this tendency among Christian singers has grown over the intervening years. I wonder what would happen today if somebody sang a song "unto the Lord" and nobody applauded. What if instead those who heard the song were so moved by it that they were stirred to seek the face of God and worship Him? Would the singer be disappointed by the lack of thunderous applause?

There was a day when men and women sought God, and because of that, they could expect God's anointing on what they were doing. There was something more in what they did, and it clutched at the hearts of their hearers. It was more than a performance. It was truly a ministry. But today, because we don't seek God and consequently don't have that anointing, we seek the approval of man.

We have even established a "Christian" organization

that exalts the talent of mere man. Every year, they give out Dove Awards, suspiciously similar to the Grammy Awards that the most talented, popular secular musicians receive. We are told that the Dove Awards are not an example of worldliness or of imitating the world, but that these awards are given to recognize the most outstanding Christian artists (incidentally, they are not usually called ministers anymore, sometimes with good reason). Those who receive these awards are quick to acknowledge God's help in fine-tuning their talent as they clutch the idol trophy they have just won. The recipient can then boast of God's touch on his life—based on how many Dove Awards he has received. They say, "We know God loves us. Look at how many times He has exalted us above other men."

Assuming for the moment that, as we are told, this exhibition is not an imitation of the world, where in the Scriptures are we told that God's servants should receive any such recognition? These awards programs actually seem contrary to the Scriptures because they honor man above God.

I believe that some of the most talented and anointed singers for God are sitting in the local Church. They don't receive cheers, fan mail or great accolades. They just sing in the Church choir, and they blend their voices with all the others so that they can take part in offering a true symphony to God.

Yet so many talented people seek fame and fortune. It is a great tragedy. Where are the plain men of God today? My heart cries out with the Psalmist.

Help, Lord, for the godly man ceases to be. For the faithful disappear from among the sons of men. They speak falsehood to one another; with flattering lips and with a double heart they speak. May the Lord cut off all flattering lips, the tongue that speaks great things, who have said, "With our tongue, we will prevail; Our lips are our own; who is lord over us?" (Ps. 12:1-4).

King David

Because of King Saul's disobedience to the Lord, God rejected Him as king over Israel. (see I Samuel 16) The Lord told the prophet Samuel that He had selected one of the sons of Jesse to be the new King over Israel. So Samuel went to Jesse and asked to see his sons. It seems that Samuel thought as most men think. When Eliab, one of Jesse's sons, passed before Samuel, the prophet assumed that he would be king because of his stature. He just looked like he would make a good king. "But the Lord said to Samuel, 'Do not look at his appearance or at the height of his stature because I have rejected him; for God sees not as man sees, for man looks at the outward appearance, but the Lord looks at the heart,'" (1 Samuel 16:7).

When Samuel finally saw David, he didn't see a great man. David was a handsome man, but he wasn't the sort of person anyone would naturally pick to be king. He was a plain man of God. He sought no glory for himself. He probably would have been satisfied with tending sheep for the rest of his life, away from the public eye. But God knew his heart, so He told Samuel, "Arise, anoint him, for this is he," (1 Samuel 16:12).

But God's anointing had been on David already, and he had done miraculous things long before anybody knew it. When King Saul was looking for someone to challenge Goliath of the Philistines, David volunteered and explained that he had killed both a lion and a bear with his bare hands, adding, "The Lord who delivered me from the paw of the lion and from the paw of the bear, He will deliver me from the hand of the Philistine."

Saul finally agreed and allowed David to go out against Goliath. But before he left, Saul urged him to go out wearing his own royal armor. Saul was not a plain man of God, and he couldn't even understand one. He couldn't understand that David's trust was in the Lord, not in earthly security blankets. Saul reverted to doing things the way man would do things, not the way God would.

When confronted with Saul's armor, David said, "I cannot go out with these, for I have not tested them." David had trusted in God, and he had tested God's armor. However, he had never put man's armor to the test. He had seen the greatest victories in his life by trusting in God's strength, not man's. So, he felt more comfortable with the strength of the Lord than with the strength of Saul's armor.

The Lesson of David

We all know the rest of the story, but we need to carefully consider David. Who was he? He was a plain man of God. He was a man after God's own heart. He was primarily a man of prayer. Most of the Psalms are prayers from David's heart. The bottom line is that David knew the anointing of God, and God knew David's heart. That combination brought down the enemy.

David serves as an example for us all. David sought his God. He had weakness, but his pursuit of God never faltered. As many times as he fell, he went right back to seeking his God. He was not a man who sought his own glory. He wanted his God, and he wanted God alone to receive the glory.

David was a man who was clothed in the armor of God, and he had learned to trust in that armor. He was a stark contrast to Saul. That King, like so many of us today, didn't seek God as he should, so he depended on his own inferior armor for coming against the enemy. But to a plain man of God like David, Saul's armor seemed strange.

Saul put his helmet on David, but it didn't fit David because he was already fitted with the helmet of salvation. The helmet of salvation protects our thinking and renews our mind. But we, like Saul, have our own inferior helmet: academia. Men who do not seek God must depend on their own ability to reason things out. But the big problem with this fleshly helmet is that it tends to preclude God's plans. Because God's ways are not our ways, His ways don't make sense to the scholar who has studied God's Word but who has not prayed. To Saul and all his men, the idea of David fighting Goliath was ludicrous. More men said that David was doomed to fail, but David, a plain man of God, said, "It's not me; it's God in me." Saul ended up losing his kingdom because he lied to God and Samuel, the prophet. But David's loins were girded with truth. He was young and innocent. All he knew was truth. And he knew truth because of all the time he spent with the author of truth.

Today we know marketing. We know how to say just the right thing just the right way at just the right moment so that people will give money. All too often we are far from being girded with truth, just as Saul was.

Saul marched in and out of many battles. His feet were shod with army boots, the best money could buy because he was the king. David's feet were shod with the gospel of salvation. But there was a more important difference between them. David's soothing music on the harp brought comfort and thoughts of God to everyone who heard him play. David wanted to bring people into God's presence. He walked as a shepherd tending the flock. Saul, on the other hand, just wanted to tromp out and do something for God.

Saul insisted that David put on his armor, but David had already put on the breastplate of righteousness. At its

174

best, Saul's armor could only stop a spear, but David's armor of righteousness protected his heart from the more serious enemies: the enemy of self-promoting, the enemy of lies, and the enemy of doubt. Those enemies had already penetrated Saul's armor and poisoned his soul because the king trusted in his armor rather than God's.

Then Saul gave David his sword, but David already had the sword of the Spirit. After Samuel anointed David, the Scriptures say, "The Spirit of the Lord came mightily upon David from that day forward." David had no use for another sword, especially a sword of the flesh. The spiritual sword he possessed already enabled him to kill a lion and a bear using only his hands. The Spirit of God can accomplish what no other sword can.

David rejected Saul's armor, knowing that he didn't need it because he already wore the tried and tested armor of God. So when he went out to confront the giant, the men of war thought he looked rather naked and helpless without any armor. Goliath had a shield bearer in front of him, but David already had the shield of faith. Goliath approached him clad with the finest, strongest armor that could be made by human hands. David approached Goliath with complete confidence in his God. It was David who won the battle, not Goliath.

When David looked at man's approach to doing God's work without prayer, he said, "This is strange to me. It doesn't make any sense. All I understand is faith. Why should you resort to feeble human tools and methods when we have available to us the power of God's Word, the sword of the Spirit, the helmet of salvation, the breastplate of righteousness, the truth and the preparation of the gospel with which to shod our feet. We already have the best of the best available to us, so why resort to man's second-rate means?"

David was a plain man of God, one of the many throughout the Scriptures who simply wanted God. They were men who accomplished great deeds through God, but brought no glory to themselves. Instead, they gave glory to God.

Polish is Not A Substitute for Power

The Church today needs plain men of God, but prayer is the only thing that will produce them. Prayer gets a man in touch with the heart of God. It gets them in touch with the mind of Christ. It puts them in touch with the way of the Spirit. From the lack of that, we have resorted to man's methods, so we are left with a lot of polish and very little power. Many preachers think that their sermons have power because they preach elequent masterpieces with great enthusiasm. But more often than not these masterpieces are full of enthusiasm, but devoid of content, and consequently possess the power of a sleeping pill.

> When I came to you, brethren, I did not come with superiority of speech or of wisdom, proclaiming to you the testimony of God...And my message and my preaching were not in persuasive words of wisdom, but in demonstration of the Spirit and power (1 Cor. 2:4).

Preaching was always meant to be a vehicle for conveying the truth of the gospel in power. But because we don't pray, we lack power in our words. We are unable to preach in demonstration of the Spirit and power. Therefore, we preach the other way, in superiority of speech. We have made preaching an art. We are in complete opposition to what Paul tells us.

Many evangelists and pastors labor very diligently to produce superiority of speech and persuasive words. They know just what stories to tell and when to pause and change the inflections of their voices in order to kindle the emotions of their hearers. They know that if they get very excited and say certain things, they can get their audiences excited. Preaching has become an art form, polished but without power. Preaching should be a demonstration of the Spirit and of power, and it will only be that as a vehicle for the gospel. The only true power we have is the power of the gospel, and we need plain men of God who will tap into it.

When a man goes to his knees and seeks the face of Him who gave him eternal life, he rises with eternity written deep in his heart. When he goes to his knees and seeks the face of the Author of love, he rises with love permeating his very being. When he goes to his knees and seeks the face of the Author of faith, he rises with a knowledge of his God that his unshakable. And when he steps to the pulpit, there is no need for showmanship. There is no need for grandstanding. There is no need for self-promoting at all. All that man needs to do is let Jesus shine forth. All he needs to do is open his mouth in power, not eloquence.

The Church needs plain men of God. If preaching is an art, it is nothing more than polish. If preaching is a vehicle for the gospel, then it is power. We need men who will preach in power, just as Jesus did.

Jesus' Way

But He Himself would often slip away to the wilderness and pray (Luke 5:16).

This reference to Jesus is so significant because it teaches us that we can pray to escape the popularity that can spawn self-promoting and preaching that is polished but powerless. Jesus had healed a leper, and the news about him was growing rapidly. Great multitudes were coming to hear him. But even in the midst of this popularity, Jesus would slip away to be with His Father because Jesus wanted to escape the popularity the crowds wanted to give him. Notice the effect that had on His ministry.

When Jesus healed people, he instructed them not to tell anyone that He had healed them. He didn't want glory for Himself. He came to glorify the Father, so he instructed them to go to the Temple and to worship and glorify the Father. Jesus was very unconcerned about revealing who He was and promoting Himself. All he wanted to do was glorify the Father.

If we want to glorify the Father, not ourselves, then we must get away and be with the Father as Jesus was. When a man does this, he realizes who he really is. Just about the time I think that I really have it all together spiritually, I slip away to pray. In that setting when it's just God and me, I am reminded of who I really am. It's like looking into a mirror long enough—it makes you realize there is nothing to glory in.

Why didn't Jesus, the Son of God, promote Himself? Because He was a plain man of God. Though He came as God's Messiah and Son, He still had only one objective in His earthly life: to glorify the Father. Jesus was a plain man of God. It wasn't a life of luxury, comfort and ease, either. He was despised and forsaken by men, a man of sorrows and acquainted with grief, and like one from whom men hide their eyes. He was despised and men did not esteem Him. That's the way Isaiah described Him. Most people today would never want to be identified like that or associated with such things.

Who has believed our message? And to whom has the arm of the Lord been revealed? (Isa. 53:1).

Everything about Jesus confused the men of His day. In essence, Isaiah was saying, "Who of us would have believed this about our Messiah, had we merely heard instead of seeing it? If we had merely heard that the Son of God had no stately form or majesty, who would have believed that He was the Son of God? We wouldn't even want to look upon Him. Who would believe that he would have an appearance that we wouldn't be attracted to?"

When Isaiah wrote, "To whom has the arm of the Lord been revealed?" "The arm of the Lord" was referring to the strength of God. Jesus had the strength of God. But if that was so, we would ask, why didn't He have an appearance that wooed every woman in the audience? If He had the strength of God, why didn't He do something to let everyone know who He was?

Jesus had one objective in life. He wanted to glorify the Father. His attention was on the Father. He came to do the Father's will. Think of how far we have drifted from Jesus' objective.

The only way to return to Jesus' objective is to return to Jesus' lifestyle of prayer.

TWELVE

Men of the Presence

Usually he is empty who is most full of himself.
—A.G. Lawson

After I spoke in the morning service, I went out with the pastor for lunch at a local restaurant where we joined several families from the Church. Both the food and the fellowship were excellent. After a few minutes, the pastor nodded in my direction and said to those around him, "He could be a mop." I quirked one eyebrow. "A what?" I asked, thinking I must have misunderstood him. "A mop," he said with a smile on his face. "What's a mop?" I asked. "It's an acronym. M.O.P. stands for Men of the Presence," he explained.

That pastor's ministry placed an emphasis on just being in God's presence. He had discipled a number of people in his Church with a similar emphasis on the importance of God's presence. He called those men M.O.P.s. It was very refreshing for me to come into a

Church that sought God, not just all the things that God could give them.

Entertainment: Surrogate Joy

In Thy presence is fullness of joy (Psa. 16:11).

The presence of the Lord is the most fulfilling thing available to us. It is the only place where we will find joy. Sometimes I think we misunderstand this verse, however. It doesn't call us to seek joy. It encourages us to seek God. When we seek joy, we usually end up drifting farther from God. But joy is not something we have to search for. God is our joy. If we lack joy, it is because of our lack of time in God's presence.

Leonard Ravenhill once said, "Entertainment is the Christian's substitute for joy." I agree. I believe that we have left God's presence and are now on a desperate search for fulfillment outside the Christian realm. That search ultimately leads us to seek out all kinds of entertainment and amusement. We justify this vain search by saying, "I am a Christian, a child of God. Therefore, God wants me to be happy." On that basis, we have rationalized doing many things that actually take us from the presence of God, and outside of His presence, there is no joy, only entertainment.

Entertainment is no viable substitute for joy. Entertainment is just some diversion that you resort to in hopes of distracting your attention away from your job, school or family. At its most basic level, it is escapism. There may be little or no joy associated with it at all. It's just something that allows you to escape from the daily concerns of life. Often entertainment's only redeeming quality is that it takes us out of the mundane.

Joy is an emotion evoked by the prospect of possessing what one desires. It is a state of happiness or bliss. In

God's presence is the fullness of joy (happiness or bliss), not entertainment. Joy doesn't depend on activities, as entertainment does. Joy, in its most beautiful expression, grows out of relationship.

Joy Through Relationship

We should be trying to develop a relationship with God. The strength of a relationship does not depend on what you do together. It depends only on being together. Close friends do not have to do something in order to be happy. Just being together is enough. This point was very aptly illustrated by my parents' regular visits to see my grandparents when I was a small boy. They always amazed me. I could never quite figure out why they would just sit around all day and talk. It seemed very boring to me. And they would do it all day long! They would sit in the living room and talk until it was time to eat, then they would move to the dining room and talk while they ate. It took me many years to realize that they just enjoyed each other's company, and they didn't have to be doing anything in particular to do that.

If my prayer life has taught me anything, it has taught me the importance of God's presence. Being with God has become the passion of my soul. There is nothing more important to me. There's nothing I'd rather do than be in His presence. It has become a compulsion with me.

One day I woke up early, and I was thinking about getting up to pray. But it was one of the few days when I had the option of sleeping in, so I decided to take advantage of the opportunity and get some extra sleep. Then I sensed the quiet, gentle voice of God say, "Don't forget about Me." "I won't," I said. "I'll have time to be with you tonight." It was the frankness and affection two lovers exchange when they speak to each other.

That evening I was at a men's retreat in Minnesota,

where I was scheduled to teach a workshop the following morning. I had flown from Milwaukee to the Minneapolis-St. Paul airport, where somebody picked me up, and we drove for two hours to Alexandria, where the retreat was. We unpacked, ate supper, I listened to the evening speaker, then had some fellowship with the guys. Before I knew it, it was midnight. I was headed to my room when I sensed that voice again. "Don't forget about Me."

My heart began to pound. It was my God calling me to His side. He was calling me to intimacy. I was sharing a room with four other men, so I couldn't pray there. Since it was so late, nobody would be out in the woods, so maybe I could...No, I couldn't pray out there. It was January and this was Minnesota. The temperature had plunged below zero. So I walked over to the tabernacle, but there were men sleeping on the floor all over the building. My heart began to sink. I couldn't find anyplace to be with my God.

Finally, after some intensive searching, I found a room that was empty. It was the room where they stored the communion utensils. It was perfect. I stepped into the room and began to give myself over to God. It was the most beautiful part of my whole day. While I was searching for that room, I had a sense of deja-vu. I had the same feeling I had when I was a teenager looking for someplace where I could get away to be with my girlfriend. It was like when I was at that awkward age when I couldn't bear for anyone to see me kiss her, so I had to sneak off to someplace where nobody could see us. But this time with God, I didn't fear that somebody would see me praying; that's not what seemed so familiar. Instead it was the expectation I experienced as I searched for someplace where the Lord and I could be alone. It was Jesus and His bride searching for a place of intimacy.

I remember the first time I met Lou Ann, the girl who was to be my wife. It was in the summer of 1974. After we had dated only once or twice, Lou Ann left for the summer to work in a camp in Ohio. I was already in love with her, but I wasn't sure how she felt about me. Then it happened. I got a letter from her, and she wrote the perfect thing: "I have thought about you a lot." That's all I needed. Just knowing that I had her attention gave me such a peace in my heart that I wanted to go right out and buy her a flower. I immediately wrote a letter back to her and said, "Since you mentioned it, I thought about you once myself." I didn't want her to think I was anxious. I was playing hard to write to.

Jesus loves us. We are His bride. He died for us, and yet we often retreat from Him like He doesn't exist. Do you ever just want to be with Him? Have you ever experienced intimacy with Him?

> You have made my heart beat faster, my sister, my bride; you have made my heart beat faster with a single glance of your eyes (Song of Sol. 4:9).

We may find it difficult to believe, but a single glance from us makes the heart of God flutter. So great and passionate is His love for us. He chose to teach us about that facet of His character by comparing it to romance between a man and a woman in the Scripture above. Do you still remember what it was like when you were in school and that person you were attracted to looked at you? I do. To me, study hall had very little to do with studying, or doing my homework, at least. It was a great opportunity for me to look at girls. And if one of them glanced at me, I was thrilled. My buddies and I would walk home, talking about the girl that looked at me (probably accidentally). All we needed was a single glance.

Draw Me

Dr. Wade Taylor has written an outstanding book about the Song of Solomon called The Secret of the Stairs. I believe that everyone should read that book at least one time. In his book, Dr. Taylor makes some very insightful observations concerning the relationship between Jesus and His bride.

Draw me after you and let us run together! The king has brought me into his chambers! (Song of Sol. 1:4).

Dr. Taylor writes, "This essential prayer, `Draw me,' relates to our spiritual hunger. Hunger is basic to all life, and finds its satisfaction in many ways. Our spiritual hunger is part of this; it must overcome and rise above the `fundamental urge of life' that is deep within us and motivates all of our actions in order to maintain itself. As we lift our desire for the Lord above all other desires, and determine that only the Lord will feed this hunger, we are truly ready to be brought into His chambers." (Dr. Wade Taylor, The Secret of the Stairs, Pinecrest Publications, p. 14).

When I first began to pray, I spent much of my time telling God that I wanted Him, that I needed Him and that I longed for Him. However, I watched a maturing in my prayer life that caused the direction of my prayers to change. At first, it scared me. Instead of telling God that I wanted Him, I began to tell God that I wanted Him to have me. At first, all I was concerned with was getting God, but as time passed, I became more and more concerned with God getting me. Now my drive and my passion is to give myself to God.

That is how the Word became flesh in my life. And that is what enables a man to preach and teach with great impact. If the Word of God has literally become his flesh, then he is truly teaching of himself. I am not saying that I have become God's Word, but rather that God's Word has become flesh to me. Through the intimacy of prayer, the two have become one. The Word of God becomes your flesh as your flesh (self) is given to God. You become His, and He becomes yours.

I often find myself counseling with someone who is really hurting, a person who feels that God is not answering his prayers. Frequently, the person's life is in turmoil with children that are disobedient, or a mate that has left. Nothing seems to be working. Many times my advice is that they stop praying about the situation and just spend time in the presence of God. They need to give themselves to God so that God can nurture them and minister to them.

Often we pray just to get more and more from God, when what we really need is to pray to give more and more of ourselves to Him. We pray and ask God to give us more, feeling that more from God is what is missing. We say things like, "If only God would answer this prayer, then things would be just right." When we hurt, we don't just need the resolution of the conflict that caused us to hurt in the first place. At those times, we need to pray prayers of unconditional surrender. We need to give ourselves completely over to God. We need to spend most of our time telling God how much we love and need Him, to express our heart's desire to draw close to Him. This level of intimacy makes you one with God.

Until the Word of God is flesh to you, it will not give you the comfort it is meant to. You can read it, study it, memorize it, but it will never accomplish in your life what it will when it becomes your flesh through intimacy with God. Today we seem to be on a desperate search for a new revelation of God. We are trying to somehow get more of God. The secret of the Kingdom is not how much of God we can get. The secret of the Kingdom is how much of you God can get. The only thing that hinders our "revelation" is what we withold from God by the refusal of dying to self.

To Life Is Christ

Paul said, "To live is Christ," and judging from what we know about his life, he meant it. But today, at best, the Church can only say, "To live is to be a Christian." We are still so immature that we are most concerned about getting all that we can out of God. Where are those who can say, "Jesus is my all in all?" The message of self-denial is all but lost in God's kingdom today. This creates a problem because Christ is not able to replace our old life with a new life until the old one dies. I learned this early in my prayer life as I was praying about a situation in which I had been very unjustly treated. I made it a matter of prayer and asked God what I should do in this situation. All God said in response was, "Ron, you must die, just die. You must die the same way My Son died."

The only way for the life of Christ to come in us is through the death of self. Christ must become our life, but that will never happen as long as we live for self. But when self is dead, then Jesus becomes our life. This is when His presence becomes our drive and desire. When self is dead, the only thing left is the life of God. Without His presence, our spiritual life ebbs away, His Word becomes stale and worship becomes rote.

To be able to pray along with Paul and say, "To live is Christ," means that you no longer live for self. There can be no self-promoting, no self-glorification or anything that takes attention away from Jesus.

I am My Beloved's

Dr. Taylor describes the beautiful progression of the bride as she pursues Christ. In Song of Songs 2:16, she states, "My beloved is mine, and I am his." In this statement, she still has an emphasis on herself first. She expresses a certain amount of self-centeredness by saying, "My beloved is mine." The focus is on herself. "...And I am his," is a secondary thought. But later, in 6:3, she says, "I am my beloved's, and my beloved is mine." Some progress is evident here. Her priorities are beginning to fall in order. Her primary thought is, "I am my beloved's." She is able to put him first. But by 7:10, she has matured even more, so that she can say, "I am my beloved's and his desire is toward me."

Dr. Taylor concludes, "Her self-life has been completely dealt with and no longer controls either her desire or her actions. Notice that there is a complete reversal of positions in the progression of these testimonies. In her first confession, she serves the Lord for her own benefit. Therefore, she said, 'My Beloved is mine." In effect, she said that she loved the Lord because He gave her the things that she wanted. This reveals a selfish or self-serving attitude towards the Lord: 'Because of the savour of thy good ointments, thy name is as ointment poured forth, THEREFORE do the virgins love thee (Song of Solomon 1:3)," (Dr. Wade Taylor, Secret of the Stairs, Pinecrest Publications, p. 26).

Finally she learned to love God for who He is rather than for what He does. She learned to love Him with no expectancy of love in return. Rest assured, beloved, that God does return our love. However, we must learn to love God simply because of who He is. When we do that, we find that skepticism is removed from our relationship with God. We no longer have any motivation to ask, "But why did this happen, God?" At this level of relationship, you realize that His desire is toward you.

God passionately loves us, and He has given all He can for us, not even stopping with the life of His own Son. Therefore, whatever God chooses to have happen in our lives should be acceptable to us because we know that God knows what is best for us. I am not talking about letting Satan dump things into our lives that God never intended to be there. But please note that the only things Satan can bring into our lives are through the flesh, and if our flesh is dead, there's no need to worry. To clearly discern between things from God and things from Satan, you need to study God's Word. But that same Word should reveal to us just how much God loves us, desires us and longs to be intimate with us, His bride. The glory of God's bride is surpassed by nothing!

More Than the Sand of the Sea

O Lord, Thou hast searched me and known me. Thou dost know when I sit down and when I rise up; Thou dost understand my thought from afar (Psa. 139:1-2).

God knows every detail about our lives. He has seen every action we have committed and every thought that has ever crossed our minds. He even knows us better than we know ourselves. He understands why we do some things even when we don't. Yet He still loves us. I once heard a man say, "God saved us not only knowing what we were, but He also saved us knowing what we would become."

How precious also are Thy thoughts to me, O God! How vast is the sum of them! If I should count them, they would outnumber the sand of the sea... (Psa. 139:17,18).

God's thoughts of us are more numerous than the sand of the sea. That is absolutely remarkable. How numerous are our thoughts about God, though? How often do we find ourselves just thinking about God?

While I was teaching a seminar in Minnesota, I felt the Lord impress upon me the need to spend five hours each day in prayer. I had gone to the Church in the afternoon to seek God. After I had prayed for some time, I was sitting in the sanctuary looking back toward the lobby. Through the glass wall, I could see the office complex. I saw many people running to and fro. The ministers were going from one office to another, from one telephone to another. It reminded me of watching an ant hill. As I was watching this, God began to gently speak to my heart about His loneliness. Not one person every took a moment to spend any time with God. God's thoughts of us are more numerous than the sand of the sea, and it seems that we struggle giving God so much as a single thought.

My ministry as an evangelist requires me to travel around the country conducting prayer seminars. I often miss my family. A day never goes by that I don't pray for them. My thoughts are with my family. But suppose God inspired me to build this great new invention that would enable me to spend time in my family's presence even when I was thousands of miles away. It would be better than a telephone because it wouldn't cost us a cent and because we would actually sense each other's presence rather than just hearing voices as we do on the telephone.

The invention has only one shortcoming: it's so big that it has to stay in my home and my family will have to operate it. I can't activate it. I can only encourage them to take advantage of it. Then suppose that I couldn't even get my family interested in this new device. I couldn't even get them to think about using it. Soon I would be facing the same problem God is.

God has provided us with the means to spend time in

His presence daily. It doesn't cost a thing, and it's better than a telephone. It's called prayer. But God cannot initiate it. We must. Do you long for His presence enough to give God time every day?

THIRTEEN

CLEAR CONSCIENCE

The world in itself has no value, it is merely zero,
but with Heaven before it, it means much.
—Baltasar Gracian Morales

A while ago, the idea of warfare prayer became very
popular. The first thing that pops into people's minds
when they hear about warfare prayer is "That involves
battle." I have no problem with that because I am absolutely convinced by the Scriptures and by experience that
prayer is a battle. However, if I talk about intercession, a
person's first thought tends to be "That's praying for
others." I have no problem with that, either, because
intercession is indeed praying for others. When I talk
about petition, people tend to respond with, "That's
praying for ourselves." That response is correct also. But,
when I consider all these correct responses together, I see
a fundamental misunderstanding.

Somehow when we think of spiritual warfare or

warfare prayer, we tend to think of it as something special or unique, a type of prayer in a class all by itself. You may determine to really engage in battle with the enemy and buckle down to do battle when you hear about his kind of prayer. However, all prayer falls under the category of warfare prayer. It doesn't matter if I'm rebuking the enemy or praying for my child. I'm engaging in a spiritual battle because all prayer is battle.

Our misconceptions and faulty ideas stem from one key problem: as a Church, we are not as interested in prayer as much as we are in battle. I have traveled all over the country for years teaching prayer seminars. The response is nominal at best. It just goes to show our lackadaisical attitude toward prayer. Christians everywhere have a ho-hum outlook on prayer. But all you have to do is attach that magic buzzword "warfare" to the ho-hum word "prayer," and everything changes.

We get excited and get ready to go into battle. We put on the whole armor of God. We gird our loins with truth. We take up the shield of faith, and we stand ready to do battle. But that's as far as we go. We're all dressed up with no place to go. You can get ready for all the battles you want, but you will never enter a single one of them until you pray.

I wonder if we get excited about Satan because he's God's archenemy. Perhaps we feel like Dr. Watson being given a chance to match wits with Sherlock Holmes' archenemy, Professor Moriarity, "the Napoleon of crime." Watson always wanted to impress Holmes, and what better way to impress him than by locking horns with the one man who considered himself Holmes' equal? Most Christians truly do want to get something done for God, and what greater opportunity than to mount some great offensive against His archenemy?

However, we need to understand that our success in battle does not depend on offensive tactics directed against

Satan. The opposite is actually true. We are on the defensive, not the offensive. Jesus Christ has already provided the victory. Walking in that victory is the most powerful thing we can do as the enemy attacks us. The greatest thing we can do in this battle is to become all God wants us to be. In the midst of that, we will see victory after victory.

Commitment to the Word or to God?

One of the greatest spiritual battles that is taking place today is between the Church's commitment to God and its commitment to the world. A man who was part of a prayer group in a small town in Minnesota told me about a vision one of the members of the group received. It clearly illustrates the seriousness of this battle. He saw two great forces, one light, the other darkness, speeding toward each other. Between these two forces was a gray buffer zone. As the two forces rapidly approached each other, the gray area between them shrunk with equal speed. He said that the gray area was where most Christians were living today. When the two forces collided, there was a tremendous explosion. The Christians in the middle burst straight up like popcorn. Then they continued to pop from one side to the other, unable to find rest on either side. They would bounce over to the dark side, but found that they couldn't live there. So, then they bounced over to the light side, but found they were unwilling to make the sort of commitment needed to live there. Back and forth they flew, not ready to settle in either place.

That vision accurately describes the predicament of most Christians today. We know that we cannot live in darkness, but we are unwilling to make the commitment it would take to live in the light. As a result we have retreated to a comfortable gray area between the two. We have adopted our theology so that it is compatible with our chosen lifestyle. For instance we justify all our worldly activities through grace. We claim that we cannot be legalists, so we must accept all things. All activities fit into the category of "Christian," or so it seems. But because we have become complacent and satisfied with living in this gray area, we have been rendered powerless against Satan.

Right now, this very second, we are in a battle. We must constantly keep in mind that this battle is a spiritual battle, not a physical one. The battle is between the light of the world and the darkness of the world. The only thing necessary to abolish darkness is to let light shine. Therefore, any identification with darkness dulls the light. The primary strategy in this battle is commitment to God. The battle is the Lord's. Therefore, the most powerful thing I can do is be committed to the Source of my strength. The opposite of commitment to God would be worldliness.

Common Sense

It seems that we no longer take a common sense look at things. We have twisted our theology around and manipulated it so that it still appears to be quite spiritual when in actuality, it is quite powerless. The Bible is full of common sense, but that common sense often threatens our current lifestyles. To some extent, I think we have tossed common sense aside in preference to lust.

My heart is grieved as I read about how today's Church spends most of its time justifying its lifestyle rather than relentlessly pursuing its God. Why aren't we spending as much time encouraging the saints to pursue God as we are encouraging them to pursue material prosperity. Why aren't we encouraging them to pray for revival and seek a life of purity as much as we are encouraging them to "eat, drink and be merry for they are the King's kids."

The greatest hindrance to revival today is not a sinful world—it's a worldly Church. As I read of the incredible revivals the United States has seen in the past, and as I see how the people in those revivals were taken up with the things of God, I realize that most of the things we are doing today would be abolished. Most of what we do is founded upon the flesh and man's ability to do things. The majority of our activity has little or nothing to do with the Holy Spirit. I would venture to say that if the Holy Spirit was removed from our Pentecostal churches today, 90 percent of what we are doing right now would continue without so much as a pause, and we would still be proud of it.

> For the wrath of God is revealed from heaven against all ungodliness and unrighteousness of men, who suppress the truth in righteousness because that which is known about God is evident with them; for God made it evident to them (Rom. 1:18-19).

Paul was dealing with a common sense problem. He said that the wrath of God is made known (to those who know God) against all ungodliness. In other words, we who know God have been given an inner sense of witness that tells us what God approves of and what He doesn't approve of. God has made it evident to us who know God the things that make up the nature of God. It's called common sense, wisdom or nature. Whatever you call it, the bottom line is that residing within all who know God is a knowledge about the nature and character of God.

> For since the creation of the world, His invisible attributes, His eternal power and divine nature, have been clearly seen, being understood through

what has been made, so that they are without excuse (Rom. 1:20).

Paul is establishing his argument against what is unnatural by causing us to see that God has given us the ability to determine what is natural, or what makes common sense.

For even though they knew God, they did not honor Him as God or give thanks; but they became futile in their speculations, and their foolish heart was darkened. Professing to be wise, they became fools (Rom. 1:21,22).

These verses are talking about God's people, for it says that "they knew God," but they didn't honor Him as God. In other words, God has revealed His divine nature to these believers, but they ignored it. Instead they became futile in their speculations—they formulated convenient theology to replace common sense. That is where the Church is today. But recall that back in Romans 1:20, we are warned that we are without excuse when we no longer do the things that make good sense.

What are some common sense issues?

Social drinking is one. Christians who drink alcohol in a nation ravaged by alcohol have failed to honor God and have become futile in their speculations of God. Does not nature itself teach us that since alcohol is tearing our country apart, to identify with alcohol in any way means that our hearts have been darkened to the nature of God?

Remember that Paul said that God has given us the ability to determine what is pleasing to God and what is not. Then he went on to address the specific sin of homosexuality. He said that one who believes that God accepts homosexuality no longer knows God. That person's heart has been darkened to what is natural. The unnatural has become natural.

I'm not talking about those who struggle with this weakness, and know that it is wrong and want deliverance from it. Everybody has some kind of struggles with sin in their lives. Paul wasn't addressing this issue. He was talking about those who have justified their lifestyle of sin. He was addressing those who were involved with sin, with the unnatural, but refused to regard it as either sin or unnatural.

When men are controlled by lust, they hide behind what Paul calls futile speculations. Instead of dealing with the lust that controls us, we justify it by twisting Scriptures around, then pasting them together. We disregard common sense completely, opting instead for our own contrived rationalizations.

We have wandered so far from the heart of God because of prayerlessness. We don't really care what God thinks about a given issue. We prefer to spend all of our time arguing with our fellow believers about the difference between grace and legalism. We ignore the fact that God has placed within each one of us the ability to discern the nature of God. The prayer life keeps that in check. The prayer life, drawing near to the heart of God, keeps our spirit tuned-in to God's Spirit.

But because we tend to abstain from prayer, we do many things in the name of Christianity that are so contrary to the life we are supposed to be living that I am grief-stricken. Prayer was always meant to be a big part of the Christian life. When it does not play a big part, we lose our sense of discernment. As Paul put it, through not honoring God, our hearts are darkened.

I am truly saddened when I think of how far we have gone from the holiness movement we have our roots in. We are not a holy people in our lifestyles. The things and activities that are unnatural in God's eyes have become natural in ours. For example, I talk with pastors who do premarital counseling regularly. They tell me that today they must assume that the Christian couple sitting before them have already had sex.

Without prayer, we lose our sense of the divine nature of God, so that all we are left with are trumped-up discussions of theology. If we can theologically justify something, we do it.

Peter's Prediction

Seeing that His divine power has granted to us everything pertaining to life and godliness, through the true knowledge of Him who called us by His own glory and excellence. For by these He has granted to us His precious and magnificent promises, in order that by them, you might become partakers of the divine nature, having escaped the corruption that is in the world by lust (2 Peter 1:3-4).

God used his divine power to grant to us His divine nature. By actually possessing the nature of God, we are able to understand that nature. That is how we escape the corruption that is in the world by lust.

Now for this very reason also, applying all diligence, in your faith supply moral excellence, and in your moral excellence, knowledge (2 Peter 1:5).

It is our business to supply moral excellence, but I don't believe that we even understand what moral excellence means anymore. As a result, I don't think we have any concern for building it in our lives. And I don't think most people even want to know what moral excellence is because, if they knew what it was, they would be unable to do many of the things they do.

Do you think that you can build moral excellence by watching nudity and profanity on TV and on movies? Is that nurturing morality in your life? Do you really believe that God is pleased when you spend His money to have Satan entertain you?

Self-Control

And let us behave properly as in the day, not in carousing and drunkenness, not in sexual prom- iscuity and sensuality, not in strife and jealousy. But put on the Lord Jesus Christ, and make no provision for the flesh in regard to its lust (Rom. 13:13,14).

Practice self-control! Rather than making provision for the flesh, put on Jesus Christ. So often, we build our lives around provision for the flesh. We structure our lives around our weaknesses. The alcoholic keeps going to the bar. The lady addicted to soap operas has a televi- sion in every room in the house. And they are dumbfounded, unable to understand why they can't kick their habits.

We need to put on the Lord Jesus Christ. When you are weak, pray. Serve notice to Satan that every time you are tempted, that is your call to prayer. Pick five mission- aries to pray for. Every time you are tempted, pray for them. This way Satan will help promote your prayer life because every time he tempts you, he will be calling you to prayer.

Watch and Pray

Keep watching and praying, that you may not enter into temptation; the spirit is willing but the flesh is weak (Matt. 26:41).

Jesus told His disciples to watch and pray. That is sound advice for us, for we are also His disciples. The word we translate "watch" is the Greek word **greegoreo.** It has to do with discernment. It means, "be on the alert, be vigilant for your life." Most spiritual warfare has to do with discernment. Discern what Satan is doing and then pray so you don't fall into his trap.

Sometimes I bring a friend with me to my seminars so that he can pray while I'm preaching. On one occasion, while he was praying, God revealed to him that a deacon in the Church we were at was having an affair with a member of the Church. We presented this to the pastor, and he confirmed that it was true. He said that they had suspected it for a long time. They had been gathering evidence. This revelation put a lid on the matter, so they began taking appropriate steps to deal with the issue.

> Put on the full armor of God, that you may be able to stand firm against the schemes of the Devil (Eph. 6:11).

Satan has a scheme. He has a plan. But Satan is a defeated foe. He tries to stir up dissension through his various schemes that can ultimately harm us. If we are not people of prayer, we will lose our discernment. If we do not watch and pray, we will not understand Satan's tactics. Without an understanding of Satan's schemes, we will get sidetracked, as I believe the Church is today.

We spend a great deal of time trying to figure out what we can do as Christians and still be saved. In fact, we spend more time in such debates than we spend going after God.

As I mentioned earlier, drinking alcohol is a popular debate among many Christians. Many drink and justify it by saying, "I won't lose my salvation and go to hell just because I drink." I'm not saying that drinking will cause anyone to lose his salvation. I can't say that. I can't judge anyone. However, involving yourself in worldly activities like that will cause you to lose the fighting edge in your battle against Satan because that edge is discernment. Through not honoring God (by being involved in worldliness), our hearts become darkened. When our hearts are darkened, we start to regard unnatural things as being perfectly natural.

I am amazed at how much discernment the Church has lost. There are so many things that believers can no longer distinguish as being Satanic in nature. Sure, we are all very excited about warfare prayer and visualizing fierce battles between angels and demons. That's all very thrilling, but we don't seem to be able to realize that worldliness is next of kin to Satan. If I am a born-again, Spirit-filled, blood-washed believer, then I should realize that any intimate involvement with the world is contrary to the life Jesus desires for me to live.

We need to realize that we are in a battle. Satan is attacking the Church and he is holding nothing back. He is expending all his energy in his assaults. Satan wants to tear down the divine nature of God within us by getting us involved in the world. He wants us to stop honoring God and to start regarding unnatural things as natural. If we cannot break away from the lusts and attractions of this world, we will be powerless to do a thing about it, no matter how much warfare prayer we engage in. Satan will win the battle if we can't let go of our love for and involvement in this world.

Warfare: Physical and Spiritual

Although our warfare is spiritual, it has physical aspects about it because prayer also has physical aspects about it. Prayer is a spiritual and physical exercise. For instance, it takes physical strength to pray, as well as faith. The physical aspects of prayer develop diligence. The spiritual aspects of prayer develop faith. However, the unique thing about prayer is that the practice of it develops both of these things in our lives. Therefore, to enter into true warfare prayer, you need both strength and faith.

> So it came about when Moses held his hands up, that Israel prevailed, and when he let his hands down, Amelek prevailed (Ex. 17:11).

During the battle against Amelek, Moses went up on a hilltop to pray. As long as he stayed in the prayer posture (hands raised in surrender), his army gained the victory. When he dropped his hands, signifying dependence on his own strength, the enemy began to win.

It takes physical strength to pray. It literally took strength for Moses to keep his hands lifted up. Aaron and Hur eventually had to come and hold his hands up. Similarly, we must exercise our strength to gain God's strength. It is not my strength against the enemy; it's my gaining God's strength.

> A wise man scales the city of the mighty and brings down the strongholds in which they trust (Prov. 21:22).

This verse perfectly describes the dichotomy of prayer. We must scale, that's the physical side of prayer. We must also bring down the strongholds, that's the spiritual side of prayer. We can learn the same lesson from Daniel who prayed for twenty-one days before the angel came with the answer to his prayer. Praying for twenty-one days requires diligence, and requires strength. Then the angel brought the answer. That was entirely out of his hands. That was the spiritual side.

We need to understand the important role that strength plays in activating faith, or the spiritual side. Because we like doing things the easy way, the way that conserves strength, we try to activate our faith without strength. We don't want to pray diligently like Daniel did. That's too much work. So we develop a doctrine that tells us we don't need strength, diligence or consistency. It teaches us to pray only once, never twice or more because to do so would be a lack of faith. It's fortunate Daniel hadn't heard of this doctrine, or he would have prayed only a minute and never seen the answer to his prayer. If Moses had bought into this teaching, he would have raised his hands in supplication for just a moment, then put them down and left the mountain while his army was slaughtered (then he would just casually brush off the slaughter by saying, "Well, they must not have had enough faith.")

Satan seems to have sidetracked us into thinking that the physical side of the battle is of no importance at all. He wants us to believe that all we have to do is exercise our faith. The fact of the matter is, we are going to need faith for the battle, but faith goes beyond just saying, "I believe that such-and-such will happen," then forgetting about it. We do need faith, but without diligence in our pursuit of God, we do not really have faith. All we have is spiritual swaggering and bombast. I think that's what we have so much of now because we have tried to remove any personal responsibility from our level of faith. In other words, we are trying to muster faith from within ourselves rather than letting it grow out of a relationship with God.

A Clear Conscience

Keeping faith and a good conscience, which some have rejected and suffered shipwreck in regard to their faith (1 Tim. 1:19).

Without a good conscience, our faith will suffer shipwreck. That presents us with a problem. As I said earlier, faith is important. We need faith in the battle we fight. Without faith, we cannot engage in warfare prayer. And where does faith come from? Hearing the Word of God, correct? But do we really hear God's Word? Have we really heard God's Word when it addresses abstinence from worldly activities?

And I don't gain faith by only hearing the Word. It's by being a hearer of the Word and a doer also. If I hear God's Word, but don't do it, I have disregarded my good conscience. In so doing, I shipwreck my faith. This explains why so many people are frustrated that their faith hasn't grown even though they have spent many hours in the Scriptures—they're hearers, but not doers of the Word. They're so involved in the world that they strive more for personal gain than for anything else.

A clear conscience comes only through consistency in my pursuit of God. If someone doesn't diligently seek God through prayer, he won't have a clear conscience in his relationship with Him.

Consider Paul's testimony before the Jewish Council. He spoke boldly because he had the great faith in God that comes from a clear conscience. He looked intently at the Council and said, "Brethren, I have lived my life with a perfectly good conscience before God up to this day," (Acts 23:1). Shortly after that, he defended himself before Governor Felix, saying,"...I believe everything that is in accordance with the Law and that is in accordance with the prophets, having a hope in God, which these men cherish themselves, that there shall certainly be a resurrection of both the righteous and the wicked. In view of this, I also do my best to maintain always a blameless conscience both before God and before men," (Acts 24:14-16).

Paul said that he thought that he had a responsibility

to live a life beyond reproach even before other men. He was able to stand trial with great confidence and say, "Here, examine my life closely. You will find nothing for which to condemn me." He wasn't afraid of have his life examined under a microscope. He had a clear conscience and nothing to hide.

If we are to have a clear conscience, then we must invite God to examine our lives. We must come to Him every day to ask Him to check our motives as well as our deeds. Have you ever noticed that when you are called upon to exercise faith, the first thing you do is ask God to search your heart? You may be praying for something for yourself, or you may be praying for someone who is ill, perhaps even on his deathbed. No matter what the issue, when we start praying for that person, we ask God to show us anything that hinders our relationship with Him. You inherently know that you must clear your conscience because if you don't, you shipwreck your faith. A very sad letter I received brought this fact a grim new dimension of reality:

Dear Brother Auch,

I do not know you personally, and I am sure that you do not know me. What prompted me to write to you was that I read your book, *Pentecostals in Crisis*. I would like to share my problems with you and pray that God will lead you and your group to pray until victory comes.

I am a minister with a wife and two children. Some years ago, I was smitten down with a disease diagnosed as Guillian Barra, a disease similar to polio. I was totally paralyzed for many months, unable to lift a finger to help myself. I am still very limited in my ability to function physically. I walk some with a walker that has wheels in front. My hands, arms, feet and legs have only a fraction of their normal use. I am very grateful to be able to walk some with the walker. I am officially totally disabled.

It has been a nightmare to me. It has been and still is almost constant pain, sometimes very severe. I have taken many kinds of tranquilizers and anti-depressants, as well as pain medicine. I am having difficulties mentally, emotionally and physically. I still preach occasionally.

I often feel guilty and fearful for not walking closer to the Lord prior to the affliction. I have repented many times, but seem to have great difficulty in praying through to real assurance and healing.

That's how the letter ended.

It's sad that this man had to go through so much to make him realize how impoverished his relationship with God was, and he was a minister. What's even sadder is that he couldn't gain a clear conscience. That's because a clear conscience isn't gained through mental gymnastics. Saying, "I repent," doesn't give you a clear conscience. A clear conscience can be gained only through a consistent pursuit of God. That's why we, like the author of that letter, are unable to pray through a crisis when we haven't had a consistent prayer life. It's not because God isn't listening to our prayers. It's because we have disregarded our good conscience, and that has shipwrecked our faith. And if our faith has been shipwrecked, we will always struggle with whether or not God is hearing our prayers.

We need to consider the words of Paul.

I thank God, whom I serve with a clear conscience the way that my fathers did, as I constantly remember you in my prayers night and day (2 Tim. 1:3).

Paul wrote that letter shortly before his death. He was in jail awaiting execution. As he reviewed his life, he had a clear conscience. He was ready to go to be with the Lord. He thanked God for his clear conscience. And what did he happen to be doing when he thanked God? He was praying constantly. And that's what we need to be doing to prepare ourselves to face life and death. We need to develop an intimate relationship with our Creator. That's the only way we'll ever be able to live lives that are holy and acceptable to God. It's the only way to sharpen our discernment and build our faith so that we can fight in the battle. And it's also the only way to live victoriously.

FOURTEEN

CLOSET PRAYER

What we do in private speaks volumes about our character. What we do in public says comparatively little.
—Rutherford Waverly

When Jesus preached his famous Sermon on the Mount, he opened the eyes of many people, showing them God's true nature and what really pleases Him. The people He was preaching to knew next to nothing about what their God actually wanted of them. That's because their teachers, the Pharisees, Saducees and other teachers of the law, had completely lost touch with their God. When they taught the people, they so thoroughly tainted God's law with their own traditions that the people hardly ever perceived Jehovah's justice or righteousness. Instead they saw only legalistic rules and regulations. Jesus, on the other hand, shared the heartbeat of God.

The difference between Jesus and the teachers of the

law was elementary: Jesus had a relationship with God, whereas the teachers of the law had only a familiarity with the letter of the law. During the Sermon on the Mount, Jesus explained that His disciples should not be like those hypocrites, "for they love to stand and pray in the synagogues and the street corners in order to be seen by men," (Matthew 6:5). Such corrupt people weren't really interested in a relationship with God, but Jesus knew that the prayer was meant to build a relationship between man and his God. So he admonished them, "But you, when you pray, go into the inner room, and when you have shut your door, pray to your Father who is in secret," (Matthew 6:6).

Many of us are more familiar with that verse as rendered by the King James Version: "But, thou, when thou prayest, enter into thy closet, and when thou hast shut thy door, pray to thy Father which is in secret." More recent translations, however, give us more insight into the original thoughts of Jesus. For example, He didn't really want us to pray in a literal closet. The word translated as "closet" is the Greek word **tamion**, which simply means a private room, one that is hidden or secret.

If we are ever going to have a strong relationship with God and a strong prayer life, it must begin with the prayer closet. I love to pray all by myself. I know of no greater joy than just getting away to be with God.

First Things First: The Prayer Closet

Before we can do battle with the forces of darkness, we must respond to God's invitation to the prayer closet. He is beckoning to each one of us to come and be with Him in the secret room. When we respond to that call, we find God as the strength of our lives in a dimension we have probably never seen before.

My wife can testify to times when I wouldn't get to

bed until 4:00 or 5:00 in the morning because I had spent the night in prayer. That's what just naturally seemed to happen when I first began to pray. I just couldn't wait to be with God. I was experiencing the greatest thing that I had ever known in my relationship with Him, and I just couldn't get enough. It changed my life, it changed my ministry, it changed my marriage.

I didn't have this kind of enthusiasm and hunger for prayer because He had answered one prayer after another. I was drawn to prayer because I knew it would mean getting to be with God, my Father, the Creator. Consequently I knew the early morning hours of the day more intimately than any other time of the day. There was once a time when God burdened me to pray for a person for three hours a day. That went on for a week. I often began at midnight. And I never grumbled about it because it was a joy and a privilege to be with my Father.

Often we overlook this simple truth. In today's busy world, we often get so busy doing the work of God that we forget about the God of the work. We'll invest hours in evangelism and outreaches, but neglect spending that precious time in the secret place with God. But what good is God's work without God? We need to slow down. We need to drop what we are doing. God is calling us aside from the cares of this world to just be with Him, to be in His presence. There is nothing more powerful than the presence of God. And if we are God's children, His presence should be the single greatest, most natural part of our lives.

Going to the Father

When my son was a four-year old he and I were in the backyard one especially pleasant summer day. I was doing some yard work. My son was playing, and I happened to notice that he had one truck on one side of the yard and several others lined up on the other side of the yard. It looked like some kind of mismatched cavalry charge was going to ensure. Curious, I asked him why he had set up his toys this way.

He picked up the lone truck and said, "This is the father. He's a farmer." Then he pointed to the other trucks facing it. "Those are his sons." Then he ran over to the group of trucks and began pushing them toward the one on the other side of the yard. "Where are they going?" I asked. He glanced up at me and then over at the lone truck. "They're going home to get something to eat," he explained. Then, after pushing the trucks "home", he made them form a huddle so they could "eat lunch".

I was deeply impressed by his words. Such innocence. In his world, he knows nothing else. In his world, if you are hungry, you go home. At that age, you don't even have to consider what it takes to put food on the table. You just show up and eat. But we all grow up, and we lose that mentality. For example, when I heard him say that the sons were going home to eat, my first thought was, "How old are they? If they're old enough to drive, then they're old enough to get their own food." It's exactly that line of reasoning that causes us problems in our relationship with God.

If only we had the attitude we had when we were four years old. If only we still believed that when we have a need, we must go to the Father; that when we are hungry, we must go to the Father. But most of us don't have that attitude. Instead we believe we have to work things out for ourselves. If we did have that child-like attitude, we would naturally go into the closet of prayer when we need our God. We would realize that prayer is the greatest call on our lives.

Our Daily Bread

Jesus continued talking about prayer in his Sermon on the Mount. He even offered a model prayer which included the words, "Give us this day our daily bread," (Matthew 6:11). There's a lot of truth in the most obvious interpretation of this verse: Jesus meant that when we're hungry we need to go to the Father. But Jesus was talking about getting more than just food. He was talking about getting God himself.

In Jesus' time, there was a widespread belief among the Jews that heaven would be enjoyed in the form of a banquet. To this day, when Jews celebrate the Passover, they still set a plate for the Messiah as a way of inviting him to be part of their banquet. It was with this in mind that Jesus instructed His followers to pray for their daily bread. Jesus wanted them to pray, "Father, come and honor us with your presence so that we can feast on you, the bread of life. Give us this day our daily fill of you. Father, we invite your presence." The Greek word we translate "bread" carries all these connotations with it, implying inviting someone's presence.

Some people have said that I over-emphasize the need for private prayer when I teach on prayer. I've been told that the Holy Spirit is already indwelling us and we are constantly living in the presence of God. Those points are all true, but when I refer to the presence of God in prayer, I'm referring to something else. You see, you can be in the presence of another person, but to be invited to be with that person is another story.

Sometimes when I travel, I'm away from home for several days. But when I finally get home, the greatest feeling in the world is my little boy running to me and jumping in my arms. He wants to be in my presence. Usually for a day or two after that, he can't get enough of me. After that, the thrill is gone, and we can go on being a normal family again. But one of the greatest feelings is that of being wanted—being invited.

A Christian can live with the Holy Spirit indwelling him, but every Christian still needs time in prayer when he invites God to be with him. No matter how long we've been Christians, we need to tell God how much we want and need His presence.

What happens when you come to God that way? You can answer that question by asking another one: What would happen if someone came to you that way? Or look at it from another point of view. If you are a parent, how do you respond when your child wants to be with you?

Our Refuge

The prayer closet is not a new idea. It predates the New Testament by several centuries.

> Come my people, enter into your rooms, and close your doors behind you, hide for a little while Until indignation runs its course (Isa. 26:20).

The subsequent verses describe the time of great tribulation on earth when judgment comes on the inhabitants of the earth for their iniquity.

I see language that is very similar when I compare Matthew 6:6 with Isaiah 26:20. In Matthew, the Lord instructs us to "...go into your inner room and...shut your door..." In Isaiah, He says, "...enter into your rooms, and close your doors behind you." The whole thought in these verses is that we are to close ourselves in with God. As we do that, He becomes our strength and our protection. It is a message with which I can personally identify.

When I was saved, I was in my early twenties. At the time, I lived with two guys in a house outside town. Our house was the local party house. We had established quite a reputation for ourselves. Just about everyone knew that if you were looking for a "good time," you should head to our house.

After I got saved, I continued to live in this house for a while, but it was unbearable. My recent salvation didn't mean my roommates had fewer parties. If anything, they had more parties, even more intense ones. It seemed like the Lord's name was used in vain in every other sentence anyone spoke. Each time I heard one of them use God's name as a swear word, it pierced my heart. I would get up and go to my room, close the door behind me and begin to call out to God. It is ironic that in the midst of all that turmoil and ungodliness that I could still draw near to God. In fact, it seems as if God was closer to me in those times of turmoil than He was at any other time.

Shutting the door was very significant. If I had just walked into my room but left the door open, I would still have been a part of the party because people from the party ended up filtering into any room with an open door. My closed door was a sign to them that I wanted nothing to do with their activities. And it was also a sign to God that I wanted nothing to do with anybody but Him. I was entering my secret place, shutting out the world, and I was inviting God to join me there. That's when God could minister to me.

Isaiah 26:20 is God's call to His people. He is calling them to shut out their turbulent, strife-ridden world, and then to come into His presence. The fact of the matter is we need the presence of God to keep us going. Our world as it is today is a fulfillment of a prophesy (Luke 21:26), for men's hearts are indeed failing them for fear. Sin is having a tremendous field day—in the world and in the Church. Yet in the midst of all this, we have a Strong Tower. While all the chaos and tension roars, we still have a refuge, and that refuge is God, and the only way to get to Him is through prayer.

Our Towers of Refuge

No matter what happens in this world of ours, God is still our refuge. He is our strong tower. However, the Bible refers to another kind of tower, the slight tower (Isaiah 5:2). The slight tower is the refuge that God's people, in our case the Church, offers. Or, at least, the slight tower should offer refuge and protection from the world. The problem is that most churches today do not offer very much protection for the saints. This is because our churches are becoming more and more worldly. The more worldly a church is, the less protection it is able to offer.

We have forgotten the significance of closing the door. We have many saints running to their churches in order to escape the world for a while, but they can't escape the world because the church door has not been shut to it. Consequently, the world follows us right into the tower. The world is in the Church today. Why? Because the Church has stopped praying. The Church has failed to enter into the closet of prayer closing the door behind.

Our only hope is prayer. We must get back to seeking God first. We must dare to go to the prayer closet and shut the door behind us—both individually and corporately. Our pleasure and entertainment must take a back seat. We must make time to relentlessly seek our God in closet prayer.

FIFTEEN

THE SPIRIT OF PRAYER

Praying is dangerous business. Results do come.
—G. Christie Swain

I often speak with pastors who share with me how they feel that they have lost their identity with Christ. It happens all too often. They once had an intimate relationship with Him through prayer, but then something happened. Their prayers lost their focus. Soon these pastors found that they talked to God only about solving all the problems afflicting their churches. What had once been an intimate relationship degenerated into a list of requests. They were no longer praying in order to get close to God. Instead they were praying exclusively that their congregations would grow larger and that the Church's problems would grow smaller.

After Dr. Cho, Larry Lee and others demonstrated the

power of prayer to produce effective, growing churches some years ago, I became concerned. It's not that I didn't agree with their teachings. In fact, I endorsed them with all my heart and still do today. I was overjoyed that pastors were finally beginning to concentrate on prayer as a result of the ministries and successes of these men. However, I became increasingly concerned that prayer might become just the latest church-growth fad, and I feared that, like all other similar fads, it would be exploited.

My house shall be called a house of prayer (Matt. 21:13).

For Jesus, prayer was pre-eminent, and it was supposed to be the central focus of God's house. But some of us have sat on church pews for so long and have heard this so often that we don't even really understand what it means for prayer to have pre-eminence. It means that prayer should have paramount rank, an austere dignity. It is supreme. Jesus said that's the kind of role prayer should play in God's house.

But under the new covenant, we are God's house. The church building isn't; that's just a meeting place for the believers. Consequently, prayer should stand out above everything else in our lives. Given this definition of the pre-eminence of prayer, I don't think many believe that prayer should be pre-eminent. This is evident by their own prayerlessness.

Do you know why prayer is to be pre-eminent? It should be pre-eminent because Jesus Christ will be the Lord of your life only to the extent to which you are willing to be with Him. He won't seize control of your life. His Lordship in your life will be directly proportional to the extent that you allow Him to be Lord over you, especially in the area of prayer.

Why do you think we have such a hard time praying? Why do you think that Satan tries so hard to prevent us from praying? It's because he knows that Jesus will only be Lord of our lives to the degree that we pray. I have always maintained that Satan wants to stop prayer more than he wants to do anything else. Once he has stopped prayer, then he can work more easily and with greater freedom at doing anything else he wants to do.

Pre-Eminent in God's House, Not in His Work

I have found that most Christians are very familiar with Matthew 21:13, but I have also found that most of them don't really understand what Jesus was getting at. I have heard many pastors ask their congregations to pray that the church would grow numerically, and they quote Matthew 21:13 to substantiate their request. These pastors know the words of Jesus, but not the substance of those words.

Remember that Jesus said that prayer should stand over and above all other things in God's house. He didn't say it should stand above all other things in God's work. Obviously, the house of God is where the work of God gets done, so there is a relationship. However, prayer is not meant to do the work of God. Instead prayer is meant to develop the house of God, and that means each one of us. Prayer should dominate our lives, and then God will be able to make us into the kind of dwelling He wants us to be.

So we should never pray just so that our church will grow. We should be praying to develop an intimate relationship with God through which God will be able to change us to make us conform more closely to the image of Christ. If we pray like this, our churches will indeed grow, but they won't grow because we pray for church growth. They will grow because of what prayer does for the pray-er. It all boils down to motive. The pastors I referred to earlier found that their motives had changed. They were no longer praying for God and what concerned Him. They were just praying for self and what concerned them.

> You lust and do not have; so you commit murder. And you are envious and cannot obtain; so you fight and quarrel. You do not have because you do not ask. You ask and do not receive because you ask with wrong motives, so that you may spend it on your pleasures (James 4:2,3).

James was writing to a rather feisty, contentious group of believers. They had wrong motives, and those motives were poisoning their relationships with each other and, rest assured, they were also poisoning their relationship with God. I believe that we, too, are having major difficulties in the area of motives. So many pastors and congregations gather only in hopes of making the size of their churches grow. Prayer was never intended as a magic elixir to pour on churches so that they would grow numerically.

We are called by God to develop an intimate relationship with Him. Nothing else. When we do that, our relationship with Him will perform God's work in our land.

> If My people who are called by My name will humble themselves and pray, and seek My face and turn from their wicked ways, then I will hear from heaven, will forgive their sins, and will heal their land (2 Chron. 7:14).

The verse above is not a call to prayer for our nation or anybody else's nation, nor is it a call to pray for church growth. It is simple. It is straightforward. It is a call to God's people to seek Him, not the advancement of their society or the cure of their societal ills. When God's people get back to earnestly seeking Him, God's work will be accomplished in their land.

The work of God is accomplished by who we are in Christ, not just by what we do for Jesus. I see Churches all across the nation that are very busy doing things for Jesus. But they are accomplishing little if anything for the Kingdom of God. Do you know why that is? It is because ministry is offering your relationship with Christ to others. If you don't have much of a relationship with Christ, you don't have much to offer others, no matter how much you do or how busy you are.

This makes us a spiritually impoverished people. But does this motivate us to seek our God, that we might know His unsearchable riches? No, not in the least. We'd rather go see what the world is peddling and drag the world's methods into the church. As a result, many of our churches are brimming over with carnality.

For example, we haul in all kinds of success principles formulated by non-Christian businessmen who have achieved great success in this world's system. Then we employ those principles to make the Kingdom of God grow, and that is a very serious error. Those principles which we esteem so greatly were designed to function in this world's system, and that is the only place where they will function. Please do not misunderstand me. The church organization needs to practice good business principles in order to operate successfully, and we are to be good stewards. But those principles just will not cause growth in the Kingdom of God. The operation of the Kingdom of God depends on good business principles, but the growth and nurturing of that kingdom do not; they depend on ministry. If you try to plug in business principles to make the kingdom grow, it's like plugging an AC socket into a

DC outlet. We should never try to mix business with ministry in this sense.

The only way to make the Kingdom of God grow is to offer the lost world the character of Jesus Christ. And let me tell you something: developing the character of Christ is not a snap, like practicing good business principles. If we are to develop that character, we must make ourselves available to God so that He can change us. The only way to do that is to offer ourselves to Him daily in prayer.

I believe the reason why we Pentecostals are having such problems today is that we have mixed business with ministry. I heard about one church growth seminar that used business principles as the primary tool for causing congregations to grow larger. The seminar highlighted such deep, insightful spiritual matters as the importance of where the bathrooms are located in your church building. Don't get me wrong. I think bathrooms are important. I use them. I would encourage every church to have them. But I am frankly astonished that we have drifted so far from the Holy Spirit that we are associating the placement of bathrooms with causing growth in God's Kingdom. The way I understand Scripture, the eternal salvation of lost souls are not dependent on how nice, numerous or centrally-located our bathrooms are. Friends, consider that all this is coming out of a movement that had its roots in the supernatural and in the Holy Spirit.

Today's Pentecostal Church has become a big business, and it is now just learning that big business has big problems. Some of our ministries would be listed as Fortune 500 enterprises if it weren't for their non-profit status. Unfortunately, we are making the mistake of treating ministry as a business. Prayer, tithing, witnessing, teaching and so on all become classified as duties we must perform in order to fulfill business principles. Our dependency on this is draining every ounce of relationship with God from our lives, and we are pouring in our culture's definitions of success and excellence into our lives to replace that relationship. The bottom line is we have developed wrong motives for what we are doing. A close study of Church history will substantiate this. Every time God brought a powerful revival, the Holy Spirit had great freedom among those who accepted and received the revival. But as the movement grew and became more organized, the Holy Spirit's freedom contracted. The more organized and structured the movement became, the more dependent the people became on their movement's growing sophistication. I believe in organization and structure, but I believe that history clearly teaches us that God's people tend to abuse those things, using them to do things that they were never intended to do, things they cannot do, things that only the Holy Spirit can do. As the Holy Spirit is squelched in favor of man's sophistication, He is able to have less and less influence. Then business principles move in and take over the ministry of the Church. Bill Gothard probably described our situation best. He said that within every business structure, there lies the seed of destruction.

We must wake up and realize that business can never grow the Kingdom of God. The only thing that grows the Kingdom of God is the Holy Spirit. The only thing that gets the Holy Spirit moving is the spirit of prayer among God's people. The only thing that gives us the spirit of prayer is the praying heart.

The Spirit of Prayer

A spirit of prayer has been described as a feeling given by God that overwhelms an individual and places a great burden of prayer upon him. Every minister and every Christian should be asking God to overwhelm him with a burden of prayer. People say, "Ron, that's fine for you. You're in the prayer ministry, but God has given me a different ministry." That's incorrect. God has first called each one of us to prayer. Remember: it is to be pre-eminent.

Every person's first call is to intimacy with God. Prayer is basic to and is the heartbeat of every aspect of ministry. Our ministry to other people must take a back seat to our ministry to God. If our ministry to God is not what it should be, then we offer nothing more than carnality to others, not spirituality. That's why so many ministries are dependent on social activities and things that feed the flesh. Outside of that, they have nothing else to offer their people.

Do We Pentecostals Even Want God?

Many people misunderstand the objective of my ministry. They think that the goal is to get people to pray. That's not really what I have in mind, nor is it what I believe God has called me to. Instead, the objective of my ministry is to get people to want God. Our problem as a movement is that we no longer want God. We want to be saved. We want to go to heaven and avoid going to hell. But we no longer want our God. We claim, often with frenzied emotionalism, that we want God, but our prayerlessness makes us out to be liars. You cannot have an intense desire for God and then continue to refuse to spend time with Him.

If we don't want to pray—I mean, really have a desire to be with God, emotions to the contrary—God will regard our prayers the way he did the prayers of the pharisees and the hypocrites, whom Jesus said made a pretense of praying, hoping their prayers would be heard because of their much speaking. I am concerned that many of our churches have lost their spirit of prayer. As a result, we may soon find ourselves going through the motions of prayer, but having little or no effect on our churches.

We need to return to the spirit of prayer. We need to come before our God with open hearts, inviting Him to be Lord of our lives. We need to establish and deepen our relationship with Him. That's the spirit of prayer, and that is what brings revival, not just prayer. It's that spirit of prayer that sustains the revival, not just prayer. The spirit of prayer is so different from grudgingly going to a prayer meeting because we know we're supposed to, then saying all the "right things" to God without opening our hearts to Him.

Private Prayer and Public Prayer

Shortly after I began Morning Manna, in our church, I was puzzled. I was praying a minimum of one hour everyday, yet there still seemed to be something lacking in my prayer life. I felt unfulfilled. That's when God began to show me the difference between private prayer and public prayer, and it was a lesson I shared with our Morning Mana group.

Private prayer is a deeply intimate experience. It is a special time of interaction between a believer and His God. That's when God develops His character in us. That, in turn, is what God uses to minister to others.

Public prayer develops God's character in the Church. A Church that prays together is more loving, more forgiving and so forth. God uses that development to minister to those He sends into the Church.

Although public prayer is crucial, it is private prayer, sometimes known as secret prayer, or closet prayer, that develops the spirit of prayer. And it's the spirit of prayer that gives public prayer its life. Without private prayer, public prayer soon loses its power and influence. The best way to tell if people are praying privately is whether or not they still enjoy public prayer. If we don't enjoy public prayer, it's because we're not getting something that we personally want out of it. Personal edification comes only in private prayer. You mustn't expect public prayer to do something it isn't intended to do. A corporate prayer meeting is not for the individual, it's for the sake of the church. It's for the sake of God's work in the community. If public prayer has replaced private prayer, it quickly drains us because then we aren't spending any time with God on our own. Charles Finney understood this, as he wrote the following:

> I am convinced that nothing is so rarely attained as a praying heart. This would be thought a strange remark...but I tell you that the church will have to get a new lesson on the subject of prayer. Frequent seasons of secret prayer...are wholly indispensable to keeping up fellowship with God. If you lose your Spirit of Prayer, you will do nothing...or next to nothing for God...though you have the intellectual endowment of an angel.

It's not just prayer that we need. It's attaining a spirit of prayer. It's secret prayer that develops the spirit of prayer within us. Once that happens, public prayer will become what it should be.

The spirit of prayer is the spirit of Jesus. Recall what Jesus did immediately after being baptized in the Jordan: He was led by the Holy Spirit into the wilderness for forty days and nights of prayer and fasting. Jesus is the one who said, "Could you not tarry one hour?" Many times, the disciples would be unable to find Jesus, only to discover later that he was in a lonely place praying to His Father. If Christ lived and grew under a spirit of prayer, can we do less?

When I first began doing Morning Manna, it was unstructured. We just came into the Church sanctuary and spent time with God alone. I believe that began to develop a spirit of prayer in the individuals who met there and in the rest of the Church. As time went along, we grew much larger in number and offered more structure to our prayer time. The results were extraordinary. I remember many visiting evangelists and missionaries telling me how they could sense the prayers of that Church. However, public prayer began to replace private prayer, and then it just became another thing to do to provoke church growth. That taught me that public prayer must never replace private prayer. Short public prayer is only made powerful through long private prayer.

Real Prayer Meetings

I frequently talk to the old-timers about prayer. They can remember the good old days when the Church had what they called a real prayer meeting. People didn't need to be coerced or prodded. They wanted to pray. The prayer meetings were packed with power. They couldn't wait to get to Church early to pray. In an average service, people were saved, healings were almost commonplace, and lives were radically changed by the baptism of the Holy Spirit. These old-timers can't understand why we don't have prayer meetings like that today.

Old-timer, you have to realize something. You were under the spirit of prayer in those good old days. The church prayer meeting was not the only place where prayer took place. You lived in a day when people prayed privately. It wasn't a day when people's thoughts were cluttered with TV. It was an era of prayer, and under that spirit, the public meeting took on an entirely different nature from what we see today. It was a day when people understood statements like this one made by S.D. Gordon: "The real victory of every service is gotten before through prayer. The service is simply gathering together the results of prayer."

Every ministry of the church will only be effective to the extent that it has been prayed for. That goes for Sunday services, children's church, the youth ministry, the singles group, care groups and the choir. Moreover, a spirit of prayer must prevail if we are ever going to see revival. I read of some of the revivals of the past and find that it was quite common to walk down the street in the middle of the day and hear people praying and weeping, groaning for the services. As long as that spirit prevailed, the revival continued. When the spirit of prayer was extinguished, so was the revival.

The strength of any move of God lies in the closet of prayer. Private, personal, intimate prayer must re-capture our hearts if we are truly going to walk in the power of the spirit.

The book, *Prayer Can Change Your Marriage*, was written for the purpose of instilling intimacy between the pray-er and God. In it, author Ron Auch, describes in detail, how to develop your personal prayer life.